I AM

DO YOU KNOW WHO YOU ARE IN CHRIST?

JAMES RONDINONE

JAMES **RONDINONE**
PUBLICATIONS

©2023 by James Rondinone

All rights reserved solely by the author. The author guarantees all contents are original and do not infringe upon the legal rights of any other person or work. No part of this book may be reproduced in any form without the permission of the author. The views expressed in this book are not necessarily those of the publisher.

Unless otherwise indicated, Scripture quotations are taken from the King James Version (KJV)-public domain.

Printed in the United States of America.

Paperback ISBN-13: 9798388525062

CONTENTS

Introduction   v

Chapter 1   1
What Does It Mean to Say That You Are in Christ?

Chapter 2   4
Was Salvation Conditional in the Old Testament Based on Obedience to the Commands of the Mosaic Law?

Chapter 3   11
Is Salvation Conditional Based on Obedience to the Commands of the Mosaic Law and/or the Directives of Those in Leadership During the Church Age?

Chapter 4   20
Is Salvation Conditional Based on the Committing of Continual Sin?

Chapter 5   37
You Are Sealed

Chapter 6   40
You Are Saved

Chapter 7   46
You Are a Child of God

Chapter 8   50
You Are an Heir

Chapter 9   53
You Are Justified

Chapter 10   57
You Are Sanctified

Chapter 11   60
You Are Perfected

Chapter 12   63
You Are Redeemed and Forgiven

Chapter 13   66
You Are a New Creature

Chapter 14   70
You Are Accepted

Chapter 15   73
You Are Washed

Chapter 16   82
You Are Dead to Sin

Chapter 17 *You Are Beloved*	87
Chapter 18 *You Are Complete*	93
Chapter 19 *You Are Righteous*	96
Chapter 20 *You Are a Peculiar Person*	99
Chapter 21 *You Are Dead to the Law*	102
Chapter 22 *You Are a Possessor of Eternal Life*	107
Chapter 23 *You Are an Ambassador*	111
Chapter 24 *You Are God's Workmanship*	118
Chapter 25 *You Are Resurrected and Seated Together with Christ*	122
Chapter 26 *You Are Healed*	132
Chapter 27 *You Are a Citizen of Heaven*	138
Chapter 28 *You Are God's Inheritance*	143
Chapter 29 *You Are Dead and Your Life is Hid with Christ in God*	148
Rich in Christ	159
Endnotes	163

INTRODUCTION

I wonder how many Christians don't know who they are in Christ. Did you know that God sees you in an entirely new way at salvation? Unfortunately, the newly converted Christians and some of those who've been saved for a while are still thinking, speaking, and acting steadily according to their former lives. Conversely, when we start attending church, whenever and wherever that might be, we're usually presented with a format for worship and accountability. This might consist of learning about the doctrines of the faith, becoming aware of the prescribed protocol for giving financially, being asked to participate in various functions such as corporate prayer, Bible study, men's or women's breakfast, teaching workshops, etc., or volunteering when needed.

Sadly, in some instances, we're unaware of all the spiritual blessings that have taken place in our lives at salvation. Instead of learning about these spiritual declarations and embracing them, we're asked to get busy and do good works for God. Therefore, our acceptance from leadership and the brethren becomes performance based. In contrast, our approval from God is based on grace through faith (repentance of our sins to God the Father and belief in His Son, Jesus Christ, as to who He is and what He has accomplished).

INTRODUCTION

Likewise, shouldn't our walk that's in accordance with the teachings of those in church leadership be founded on grace through faith?

This study will bring awareness of who we are in Christ to our attention, which is another way of saying that this is how God sees us and, conversely, how we should see ourselves. When we realize who we've become and how precious we are in God's eyes, striving to please Him, church authority, or our spiritual peers that's based on achievement will be questioned. And hopefully, we'll be guided to serve because our motivation is founded on the correct perception of ourselves and others as revealed by God's Word.

Are you ready to discover the many truths about yourself that can't be undone by anything you think, say, or do?

This doesn't mean that grace is a license to sin. It simply means that what grace provides, sin can't undo or affect. Grace remains grace. The new you will stay the new you.

In most of the following chapters, I'll present one established irrevocable fact about your new standing in Christ. Are you ready to learn about each one of them? I am. Along with this, certain questions will be asked in some chapters so that you'll fully understand the certainty of your salvation. Are you ready to begin? Let's go.

1

WHAT DOES IT MEAN TO SAY THAT YOU ARE IN CHRIST?

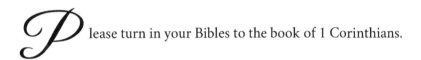lease turn in your Bibles to the book of 1 Corinthians.

1 Corinthians 1:30

> *But of him are ye in Christ Jesus, who of God is made unto us wisdom, and righteousness, and sanctification, and redemption:*

Did you know that it's of God the Father that you have a spiritual existence? Concerning such [you were] born again by the grace of God in Christ[1] (by living in union with Him[2]). Furthermore, Christ is the source of the following spiritual blessings. Who was *made unto us wisdom* from God - both righteousness and sanctification and redemption.[3]

So, what does it mean when Scripture declares that we're *in Christ*?

It *means that when we believed the gospel, we were placed in union with Him.* And because of such we have received the blessings of *righteousness* (put right with God), *sanctification* (set apart to belong to

God), and *redemption* (free from the ramifications of sin owed to satisfy the justice of God).

By the way, did you know that all of these blessings and much more have been produced in you through another special member of the Trinity? Do you know the name of who this might be? Well, the following verse will not only tell us so but will reveal to us the purpose of these blessings.

> *Ephesians 1:3 Blessed be the God and Father of our Lord Jesus Christ, who hath blessed us with all spiritual blessings in heavenly places in Christ:*

God the Father has *blessed* (benefitted) *us with all spiritual blessings* (Spirit-produced blessings; every spiritual enrichment needed for the spiritual life,[4] since these benefits have already been bestowed on believers, they [shouldn't] ask for them but rather appropriate them by faith[5]) *in heavenly* (in the heavenlies; to prepare for heaven[6]) *places* (not in the original manuscripts) *in Christ.*

By the way, when we take a closer look at the words of the verb *hath blessed,* which is in the form of an aorist active participle in **Koine Greek**, the language by which most of the New Testament was written, here's what else they reveal to you. The **tense** tells us what kind of action is expressed by the verb. There are seven tenses: aorist, present, future, perfect, imperfect, future perfect, and pluperfect. Of these, the most common occurrences will be the present tense which denotes continuous action in the present; the perfect tense, which expresses action completed in the past with present results; and the aorist tense, which denotes action occurring at a point in time. In this instance, the tense is aorist which declares that you were blessed at a point in time, i.e., when you believed the gospel.

Something else to keep in mind is the voice. The **voice** tells us how the subject is related to the action of the verb. There are three voices: active, middle, and passive. The active voice tells us that the subject produces the action. The middle voice indicates that the subject both produces and receives the action. And the passive voice points out that the subject receives the action. In this instance, you received the action of being blessed by God the Father.

Another thing about a verb, even though it's not mentioned here, is the mood. The **mood** is how the action of the verb is conceived regarding reality, which can either be actual or possible. There are four moods: indicative, subjunctive, imperative, and optative. The moods that are most often used are the indicative, which tells us that the action of the verb is of certainty or fact, and the subjunctive, which denotes possible action of the verb if certain existing facts take place.

And finally, what we have here is what is called a participle. A **participle** is a verbal adjective that tells us why someone is doing something or why something is being done. We can surmise why God the Father has blessed you. This is because you responded to the gospel of Christ and have received the originator of these blessings, i.e., the indwelling Spirit.

With that said, we're almost ready to take a look at the blessings that are Spirit-originated. *But before we do, you should be aware of the view of some who proclaim that salvation can be lost.* If this is true, then the blessing of the indwelling Spirit, along with additional ones, are conditional. Could this be true? There are three views that espouse this perception. Let's begin by looking at the first one in the following chapter that has to do with the Mosaic Law.

2

WAS SALVATION CONDITIONAL IN THE OLD TESTAMENT BASED ON OBEDIENCE TO THE COMMANDS OF THE MOSAIC LAW?

*B*efore we take a closer look at salvation for the New Testament saint, we should define it. *Salvation is the bundle of benefits received by the person who believes the gospel and entrusts [their] life to Christ.*[7] Some of these privileges are receiving the indwelling Spirit, becoming a new creation in Christ, being declared holy and beloved, and many more. However, does this have the same meaning for an Old Testament saint? Let's find out.

In the Old Testament, during the dispensation of the Age of the Jews, they were supposed to obey God (*Yahweh*) by obedience to the commands of the Mosaic Law. What is the Mosaic Law, you ask? The Mosaic Law was an institution conveyed to Moses by God. The various aspects of this Law could be described by using four words.

- **Statutes** - the Spiritual Code or the ordinances of the Law (e.g., the Tabernacle, the Holy Days, the Sin Offerings, the High Priest, the Meat Offering, the Trespass Offering, the Levites, etc. - Exodus 26-31; 35-40; Leviticus 1-24; Deuteronomy 16).
- **Commandments** - the Moral Code, which included not

only the ten commandments called the Decalogue (e.g., honor thy father and thy mother…Exodus 20:12-17) but six hundred thirteen other commandments (e.g., thou shalt have no other gods before me; the Sabbath, … thou shalt not do any work … Exodus 20:12-17; Deuteronomy 5:6-21; Deuteronomy chapter 12).
- **Judgments** - the Social Code, which are the laws belonging to civil government, e.g., dietary, marriage, military, conservation, etc., along with the related punishments (Deuteronomy chapters 14-28).
- **Testimonies** - the laws directing the commemoration of certain events (e.g., the Seventh year Sabbath rest, the fiftieth year of Jubilee, the ordinance of the Passover, the feast of unleavened bread, etc. - Exodus 12:43-50; Numbers 28:16-25; Deuteronomy chapters 25-26).

It's true that under this institution, various commands were clearly delineated. And disobedience to any one of them would result in various degrees of ramifications. *Did you know that there are many Christian churches that choose not only to ask the congregation to obey some of the tenets of the Mosaic Law, such as observing the seventh day Sabbath, obeying the ten commandments, and tithing, but they also believe that obedience to whatever else they ask of them forms the ground for maintaining or securing one's salvation?* Some of the avenues that believers are expected to participate in are corporate prayer, Bible studies, volunteering, faithfully attending worship services, etc. *While there's nothing wrong with being involved in any of these, does the decision of any believer to not be engaged in any of such endanger their salvation?*

Before we attempt to answer this question, let's find out the answer to the following one. *What caused someone in the Old Testament to be saved?* Please turn to the book of Romans.

Romans 4:3 For what saith the scripture? Abraham believed God, and it was counted unto him for righteousness.

This tells us that *Abraham believed God* in His promise that his posterity should be like the stars of heaven.[8] And because of which *it* (believing His Word) *was counted unto him* (put to his account) *for righteousness* (as one who was admitted to the favor and friendship of God[9]). *So, believing in God's Word is synonymous with believing in God (Yahweh) was the basis for salvation. However, salvation in this dispensation meant going to a compartment (Abraham's bosom) in hell at physical death (Luke 16:19-31).*

With that said, any idea what was the protocol for walking with Yahweh for the ancestors of Abraham who believed in Him? The obligation was for them to serve the Lord by means of obeying the tenets of the Law that He conveyed to Moses. Well, what if some of them continually chose not to obey the Law? Did they lose their salvation? Some would say most certainly, as evidenced by the life of one of the kings of Israel named Saul. Who is Saul?

He was Israel's first king. His reign was marked by military victories over Israel's enemies, but unfortunately, at times, he exhibited character traits that weren't of divine orientation. While no one is perfect, he didn't seem to learn from his decisions that emanated from human viewpoint. One might assume that he neglected to spend time in the Torah (the first five books of the Bible), learning and appropriating God's commands, judgments, testimonies, and statutes.

This was evident in so many instances. In one example, when the Israelite army was engaged in a battle with the Amalekites, he was instructed by the prophet/judge Samuel to kill all the people, their King Agag, along with all of their livestock. Saul, to his own detriment, obeyed this admonition as he saw fit. He spared the king and the choice of livestock. Was he disciplined for his disobedience? And if he was, by whom?

> *1 Samuel 16:1 And the Lord said unto Samuel, How long wilt thou mourn for Saul, seeing I have rejected him from reigning over Israel? fill thine horn with oil, and go, I will*

> *send thee to Jesse the Bethlehemite: for I have provided me a king among his sons.*

After this incident, the Lord told Samuel that He had rejected Saul from reigning as king and that one of the sons, i.e., the youngest named David of a man named Jesse, would succeed him.

> *1 Samuel 16:14 But the Spirit of the Lord departed from Saul, and an evil spirit from the Lord troubled him.*

Not only would another take over the kingship, but God caused *the Spirit* (who works upon men as the spirit of strength, wisdom, and knowledge, and generates and fosters the spiritual or divine life[10]) to depart (the on-resting Spirit, not an indwelling Spirit) and instead *an evil spirit* (a supernatural evil spirit) *troubled* (influenced) *him*. This poison spirit not only deprived him of his peace of mind, but stirred up the feelings, ideas, [imaginations], and thoughts of his soul to such an extent that, at times it drove him even into madness.[11]

If we were to leave this story as is, then we might conclude that an Old Testament saint could lose salvation based on habitual disobedience to God's commands. But wait, the rest of the story is yet to be told. As time went on, King Saul's behavior continued to deteriorate until it caught up with him at his most desperate hour. Please turn to the book of 1 Samuel, and we'll find out what this was all about.

> *1 Samuel 28:1a, 4-6 And it came to pass in those days, that the Philistines gathered their armies together for warfare, to fight with Israel... And the Philistines gathered themselves together, and came and pitched in Shunem: and Saul gathered all Israel together, and they pitched in Gilboa. And when Saul saw the host of the Philistines, he was afraid, and his heart greatly trembled. And when Saul inquired of the Lord, the Lord answered him not, neither by dreams nor by Urim, nor by prophets.*

Unfortunately for King Saul, his day of reckoning has now arrived. And he's in a predicament. A battle between Israel and one of their chief enemies, the Philistines, was about to take place. So, he decided to go up to a high place to get a better view of their company and realized that this wasn't going to end well.

Even though his relationship with God had been nonexistent for a long while, he sought to inquire counsel from Him through various means (e.g., dreams, prophets, and Urim, i.e., the Urim and Thummim which were two stones that were kept within the folded breastplate of the high priest that somehow were used to determine the will of God for the nation) probably figuring that he had nothing to lose. However, God chose not to provide him with any direction.

> *1 Samuel 28:7 Then said Saul unto his servants, Seek me a woman that hath a familiar spirit, that I may go to her, and inquire of her. And his servants said to him, Behold, there is a woman that hath a familiar spirit at Endor.*

Being desperate, he resorted to seeking out *a woman* who had *a familiar spirit*. She was otherwise known as a medium, one who was possessed by an evil spirit. The phrase *familiar spirit* indicate that she could call up departed spirits to give answers to those who consulted them.[12]

Even today, there are apparently people who claim that they can confer with the dead. This begs the question. Just who are these departed spirits that are being referred to here? Some say they're the spirits of people who did or didn't believe in God when they lived on the earth and subsequently, after they died, went to one of two places in hell. For believers in *Yahweh*, they went to a place called Abraham's bosom. For unbelievers, they went to a place called torments (Luke 16:19-31). Others believe that these aren't the spirits of the dead at all but are demons (fallen angels) who are impersonating the dead. Well, the following verses tell us who these spirits were, at least in this particular instance.

> *1 Samuel 28:16, 19 Then said Samuel, Wherefore then dost thou ask of me, seeing the Lord is departed from thee, and is become thine enemy? Moreover the Lord will also deliver Israel with thee into the hand of the Philistines: and to morrow shalt thou and thy sons be with me: the Lord also shall deliver the host of Israel into the hand of the Philistines.*

The medium proceeded to ask King Saul who he'd like to hear from. And he replied Samuel. When she saw him appear, she cried out as if in shock, possibly because Scripture told us that she recognized the person who was asking her to get in touch with him, who was actually Saul, the king of Israel. Samuel proceeded to ask the king why he summoned him. Saul replied because he'd attempted to receive direction from the Lord as to the state of affairs relating to the upcoming battle with the Philistines, and He chose not to reply.

Samuel said that the reason God had chosen not to confer with him was because of his continual disobedience to His directives. However, God did allow Samuel to give him the bad news, i.e., Israel wouldn't only be defeated, but both himself and his sons would be killed. And besides conveying this, he made a startling statement. And that was that all of them would be with him where his spirit resided, which was at the place called Abraham's bosom.

What we can conclude is that a believer's walk with the Lord in the Old Testament consisted in not only obeying the tenets of the Mosaic Law but also obeying leadership when they received verbal instructions from the Lord. This begs the question. If an Old Testament saint chose to live in continual disobedience to God's commands, would they lose their salvation? As evidenced in the story just presented, the answer is no.

So, where do we go from here?

What we'll take a look at next is known as the new covenant, the covenant of grace and truth, which was unveiled in the dispensation known as the Church Age, the age in which we currently live. What we'll find out are the answers to some of the following questions.

What is the basis for someone becoming saved?

Is disobedience to the commands of the Law or the commands of those in church leadership the basis for a New Testament believer losing their salvation?

Let's find out by turning to the next chapter.

3

IS SALVATION CONDITIONAL BASED ON OBEDIENCE TO THE COMMANDS OF THE MOSAIC LAW AND/OR THE DIRECTIVES OF THOSE IN LEADERSHIP DURING THE CHURCH AGE?

*W*ell, here's a million-dollar question for you to consider. *Is continual disobedience to various aspects of the Mosaic Law and/or church-related directives the basis for the removal of the indwelling Spirit along with the Spirit-produced blessings at salvation during the Church Age?* To answer this, we need to look at what forms the basis for the new covenant that followed the Mosaic Law, which is called the compact of grace and truth.

> *John 1:17 For the law was given by Moses, but grace and truth came by Jesus Christ.*

What we know about the Mosaic *law* that *was given by Moses* are a few things. It [provokes sin] and excites the passions [that] it punishes.[13] It was a Divine bestowment of entirely unspeakable value to those who were ignorant of the mind and will of God.[14] It was but "a figure for the time then [present] that [couldn't] make the worshippers perfect as pertaining to the [conscience,] because it [wasn't] possible that the blood of bulls and of goats should take away sins" ([Hebrews] 9:9; 10:4).[15] It also had a shadow of good things to come, though not the very image of the things ([Hebrews] 10:1); and it was this shadow of Gospel blessings which was given by Moses.[16]

On the other hand, the new covenant of *grace and truth came by Jesus Christ*. What is *grace*, you ask? *Grace* is God's favor and kindness bestowed on those who [don't] deserve it and cannot earn it.[17] With that said, what is *truth*? *Truth* refers to the life, death, and resurrection [of Christ, who] met all the demands of the Law, [and] now God is free to share [the] fullness of grace with those who trust Christ.[18] Another way to define *grace and truth* is to say they're the highest manifestation and self-communication of Divine love and Divine thought, [which] came into human experience through Jesus Christ.[19]

What we can now attempt to answer in this dispensation is the following question. *What constitutes salvation?*

> *Acts 17:30 And the times of this ignorance God winked at; but now commandeth all men every where to repent:*

> *John 3:14-15 ... the Son of man ... That whosoever believeth in him should not perish, but have eternal life.*

> *John 7:38-39a He that believeth on me, as the scripture hath said, out of his belly shall flow rivers of living water. (But this spake he of the Spirit, which they that believe on him should receive:...*

> *Ephesians 2:8 For by grace are ye saved through faith; and that not of yourselves: it is the gift of God:*

These verses tell us that the basis for an unbeliever becoming saved in this dispensation is that they must repent and believe in His Son Jesus Christ, who pre-existed time, came to earth, i.e., God incarnate (God come in the flesh), was born of a virgin, never sinned, listened to and obeyed the directives of God the Father, died on a cross paying the debt owed by mankind for the sins of the world, forgave sin (canceled or wiped away the record), rose again after three days never to die again, and ascended into heaven to be seated at the Father's right hand.

When God the Father witnesses an unbeliever's confession about their sinful state and their professed faith in His Son, the third member of the Trinity, the Holy Spirit will come into their life, thus indwelling their body. *While many churches believe in an unbeliever's admission of sin, their response to the gospel of Christ, and the receiving of God the Holy Spirit, they'd contend that this salvation is conditional, i.e., it's based on obedience.* Obedience to what or whom? Let's find out by turning in your Bible to the book of Hebrews.

Hebrews 5:9 And being made perfect, he [Christ] became the author of eternal salvation unto all them that obey him;

As church leaders declare that they operate in Christ's stead, so they contend that eternal salvation is secured only by those in the congregation who obey them, i.e., likewise, as those who are obeying Christ. This obedience is in regard to whatever those in church leadership declare that the assembly should be obedient to. This begs the question. *Is obedience the basis for a believer maintaining their salvation? I'd suggest that there's a different way of describing maintaining one's salvation, which is called sanctification.* What does this mean, you ask? Let's take a look at a verse from the book of 1 Thessalonians and find out.

1 Thessalonians 4:3 For this is the will of God, even your sanctification, that ye should abstain from fornication:

The Apostle Paul was instructing the believers at Thessalonica as to what the *will of God* is, and, i.e., it's in regard to a process called *sanctification* that would help them *abstain* (become completely set free) *from fornication* (sexual immorality). Are you aware that there are two aspects to sanctification? The first work consists in cultivating the positive principles of holiness in the soul.[20] The second involves overcoming the propensities to evil in our nature, checking and subduing the unholy habits which we had formed before we became Christians[21] by applying the principles that were initially learned. What are these principles? They're found in the book of Galatians. Please go there in your Bible.

> *Galatians 5:22-23 But the fruit of the Spirit is love, joy, peace, longsuffering, gentleness, goodness, faith, Meekness, temperance: against such there is no law.*

So, we could say that sanctification is learning how to think about ourselves, others, and the circumstances of life by cultivating the fruit of the Spirit. It's not obedience to rules, ceremonies, rituals, or demands but learning how to develop godly character, which is explained to us in the book of Romans.

> *Romans 12:2 And be not conformed to this world: but be ye transformed by the renewing of your mind, that ye may prove what is that good, and acceptable, and perfect, will of God.*

What helps us in this endeavor is by focusing on being *transformed by the renewing of your mind*. The Apostle Paul was strongly urging the believers at Rome to not be *conformed to this world*. The word *conformed* means to not put on the form, fashion, or appearance of. The appearance of what? The appearance of the *world*. The word *world* means the standards of the world; as much opposed to the spirit of genuine Christianity.[22]

But rather *be ye transformed by the renewing of your mind*. The word *transformed* means to appear as new persons with new habits. How is this accomplished? This is cultivated by practicing *the renewing of your mind*.

What these words refer to is a complete change for the better of the believer's mental processes. Another way to put this is that God transforms our minds and makes us spiritually minded by using His Word. *As you spend time meditating on God's Word, memorizing it, and making it a part of your inner man, God will gradually make your mind more spiritual.*[23]

When we confess known sin and learn and apply God's perspective about any area of weakness, we'll be operating under the rule of the Spirit. And thus, as the Spirit agrees with what we're occupied with in our mental attitude, He co-labors with us. *This conveys to us that sanctification is not in dos and don'ts but in viewing all aspects of life from divine perspective. Therefore, the inference that the word obey, or being obedient to God's commands, whether those contained in the Mosaic Law or those of church leadership in Hebrews 5:9, somehow secures a believer's salvation must mean something else.* What else it could mean is found in the book of 2 Thessalonians. Please turn there.

> *2 Thessalonians 1:8 In flaming fire taking vengeance on them that know not God, and that obey not the gospel of our Lord Jesus Christ:*

> *Romans 1:16 For I am not ashamed of the gospel of Christ: for it is the power of God unto salvation to every one that believeth; to the Jew first, and also to the Greek.*

The Apostle Paul declared that those who *know not God* are those *that obey not the gospel of our Lord Jesus Christ.* We're also told in the book of Romans that this same gospel *is the power of God* (God's spiritual dynamite), which breaks the granite-like heart of the sinner *unto salvation* (the complete deliverance from sin and eternal death) *to every one that believeth* in it. So, we can surmise, therefore, that the word *obey* means *believeth*. With these thoughts in mind, Hebrews 5:9 could be rewritten as such.

> *And being made perfect, he [Christ] became the author of eternal salvation unto all them that [believe in] him;*

Now that we know that it's not obedience that secures one's salvation, another thing we need to make known is that there's a clear distinction between salvation and sanctification. Let's begin with salvation. Did you know that salvation occurs at a point in time? It's based on a one-time decision. The book of Ephesians will clarify this for us.

> *Ephesians 2:5 Even when we were dead in sins, hath quickened us together with Christ, (by grace ye are saved;)*

No matter whether someone is spiritually dead in their soul in sin, God the Father will quicken them (make alive; spiritual resurrection; the impartation of divine life) by means of the Holy Spirit *together* (in union) *with Christ,* for *by grace* (a mercy that is rich, exhaustless[24]) you *are saved* (by repentance and belief the new believer is justified, i.e., the removal of the guilt and penalty of sin and the impartation of a positive righteousness[25]). And along with this, positional sanctification has taken place. *Positional sanctification? This refers to the act of the Holy Spirit taking the believing sinner out of the first Adam with his sin and [death] and placing him in the Last Adam (Jesus Christ) with His righteousness and life.*[26]

With what we've already learned, some might continue to say that this *new standing in Christ* is conditional based on obedience to thus and such. Well, did you know that the word *saved* in Koine Greek is in the form of a perfect passive participle? The perfect tense refers to action completed in the past with present results. So, here's what this is saying to us. When you responded to the gospel in the past, you received a saved state which continues on in the present.

So, your salvation, your saved state, and your positional sanctification are secure and not dependent on another way to describe sanctification, that's called progressive sanctification. What is progressive sanctification? This pertains to a believer's walk with God in time. It's the process by which the Holy Spirit eliminates sin from the experience of the believer and produces His fruit, gradually conforming him into the image of the Lord Jesus.[27] This is found in the book of Galatians.

> *Galatians 5:25 If we live in the Spirit, let us also walk in the Spirit.*

If we live (wherein we are continually alive though sometimes inactive;[28] the new divine life resident in their beings[29]) *in the Spirit, let us also walk in the Spirit* (to conduct themselves under the guidance, impulses, and energy of that life[30]). The word *walk* in Koine Greek is a present active subjunctive. The present tense denotes continuous action in the present. The active voice indicates that the subject produces the action. And the subjunctive mood denotes possible action of the verb if certain existing facts take place. Putting these together, here's what we could deduce.

Whether these believers continually walk in the Spirit is a decision they'll have to make. *Exercising judgment to grow spiritually is a choice that each of us must determine on a daily basis. Therefore, progressive sanctification is conditional. This confirms that salvation is once and for all and is not affected by the choices a believer makes in time.*

There are those who still might believe that obedience to the Mosaic Law or whatever leadership says that's needed to be obeyed in order to secure one's salvation is supported by a verse that's found in the book of Hebrews. Please turn there.

Hebrews 13:17 Obey them that have the rule over you, and submit yourselves: for they watch for your souls, as they that must give account, that they may do it with joy, and not with grief: for that is unprofitable for you.

The Jewish converts to the Christian faith were asked to *obey* (follow their orders; do what they tell you to do) *them* (the overseers or leaders of Christian churches) *that have the rule* (authority) *over* them *and submit* themselves (yield themselves trustfully to their teaching;[31] submit to their authority in all matters of doctrine and discipline[32]). *Based on the way this verse was translated, it appears that those in church leadership are to be obeyed and submitted unequivocally by the congregation. Is this true?* A verse from 1 Peter will help to clarify this.

2 Peter 2:1 But there were false prophets also among the

> *people, even as there shall be false teachers among you,*
> *who privily shall bring in damnable heresies, even denying*
> *the Lord that bought them, and bring upon themselves*
> *swift destruction.*

This clearly tells us that some in leadership can be described as *false prophets* or *teachers*. So, should we be submissive to what they have to say? Absolutely not! How can we discern such? 1 Timothy is where we'll go next.

> *1 Timothy 3:1-7 1-2a This is a true saying, If a man desire the office of a bishop, he desireth a good work. A bishop then must be ...*

If someone wants to be a leader in the church, then there are qualifications that need to be met. And there's something else we should be aware of concerning those in church administration that a few verses in 1 Peter will unveil to us.

> *1 Peter 5:1-3 The elders which are among you I exhort, who am also an elder, and a witness of the sufferings of Christ, and also a partaker of the glory that shall be revealed: Feed the flock of God which is among you, taking the oversight thereof, not by constraint, but willingly; not for filthy lucre, but of a ready mind; Neither as being lords over God's heritage, but being ensamples to the flock.*

Besides the qualifications, there are elements of Christian character that should be evidenced to the congregation.

With that said, let's take a closer look at something that was mentioned in the verse from Hebrews 13:17 that's of paramount importance as to what should be one of the main focuses of the ministry for those who are in church authority, i.e., they should *watch for your souls*. The word *watch* means to exercise constant vigilance over. Over what?

Obedience to the Mosaic Law? No. Obedience to rules and commands? No. But rather over continuous concern *for your souls*. The word *souls* can mean the salvation of the [people, and] all the arrangements should be with that end.[33] It also characterizes a person in the comprehensive [thorough understanding of vitality (the power to live or grow];[34] [mental vigor] through which he really is himself.[35] Did you get what was just said? The following verses will clarify.

> *Colossians 3:10 And have put on the new man, which is renewed in knowledge after the image of him that created him:*

> *Romans 8:29 For whom he did foreknow, he also did predestinate to be conformed to the image of his Son, that he might be the firstborn among many brethren.*

That is what all of the doctrines of the Christian faith should be, i.e., to this end, to know who we are in Christ and be conformed to the image of God's Son. This should be the main reason why we obey those in church leadership. And the rest will take care of itself.

Well, there's one more reason that some are convinced will cause a believer to lose their salvation. What is it, you ask? The next chapter will disclose this.

4

IS SALVATION CONDITIONAL BASED ON THE COMMITTING OF CONTINUAL SIN?

Some believe that a Christian can lose the indwelling Spirit along with additional blessings if they choose to live in habitual sin. There could be five reasons that they base their reasoning. Let's take a look at each one.

•The on-resting Spirit

In the last chapter, we learned that the Holy Spirit departed from King Saul because of habitual disobedience to God's commands. Prior to his death, before an upcoming battle with the Philistines, it was revealed to him that his spirit would reside in the same place the prophet/judge Samuel, who was summoned by the witch of Endor at the king's request. As we'll see in a verse from the book of Psalms, there was another king that was concerned with the on-resting Spirit departing from him.

> Psalms 51:11 *Cast me not away from thy presence; and take not thy holy spirit from me.*

Even King David asked God not to take away the Spirit from him because of his decision to commit adultery with a woman named Bathsheba, along with having her husband Uriah killed in battle.

What we've learned from the Old Testament was that the Spirit influencing a believer was on-resting (temporary) and not indwelling (permanent). His effects were conditional based on whether the respondent continually rejected God's directives. But this didn't affect an Old Testament saints' salvation which was based on believing what God or in Him as He revealed himself (James 2:23).

The idea of what salvation meant in the Old Testament was that a believer would go to a place in hell upon physical death called Abraham's bosom. Those that didn't believe in Him would go to a different compartment described as torments. Abraham's bosom was a temporary place where the God-believed spirits of the human dead resided. Are these spirits still there? A verse from the book of Ephesians will clarify this.

> *Ephesians 4:8 Wherefore he saith, When he ascended up on high, he led captivity captive, and gave gifts unto men.*

Scripture indicates that following Christ's resurrection, when *he ascended up on high*, the spirits of the human dead that resided in Abraham's bosom accompanied Him to heaven. *What we can conclude is that the on-resting Spirit did leave a believer because of perpetual sin, however, their salvation remained secure.*

- The forgiveness of sins

> *1 John 1:9 If we confess our sins, he is faithful and just to forgive us our sins, and to cleanse us from all unrighteousness.*

Some believe when Scripture says that we must *confess our sins* to God the Father so that He would *forgive us* of them; this is because all sin wasn't forgiven at the cross. Therefore, if a believer continues to commit sin and doesn't confess them, then they'd lose their salvation. Is this scripturally accurate? Please turn to the book of 1 John, and we'll find out.

> *1 John 2:1 And he is the propitiation for our sins: and not for ours only, but also for the sins of the whole world.*

First of all, Jesus *is the propitiation* (the atoning sacrifice) *for* the *sins* of believers and unbelievers alike, having paid the penalty, thus appeasing or satisfying the wrath of God whose standard had been violated.[36]

But what about the forgiveness of sins concerning us who are saved?
Let's go to the book of Ephesians.

> *Ephesians 1:7 In whom we have redemption through his blood, the forgiveness of sins, according to the riches of his grace;*

Second, all of our sins were forgiven on the cross prior to when we repented and believed in Christ. This verse beautifully states that *in whom* (Christ) *we have redemption* (to let one go free; separation from all of the consequences of our transgressions) from the judgment of all our sins *through his blood* (the price paid to divine justice) and *the forgiveness* (to blot out; not to remember any longer; to throw a person's sins behind one's back; to carry away our sins so that they might never again be seen) *of sins.*

The verb *have* in Koine Greek imply that because we had repented of our sins and believed in Christ, we are subsequently *in whom* (in Him). Furthermore, this is in the form of a present active indicative. The indicative mood tells us that the action of the verb is of certainty or fact. *What this tells us is that every believer has redemption and forgiveness continuously in effect in their new life that's in union with Christ.*

If this is the case, then why do we need to confess known sins to

God the Father? Good question. In 1 John 1:9, we're told that when *we confess our sins*, He chooses *to forgive us our sins*. The word *forgive* means a few things, such as to remove discipline (chastisement) from God the Father, to recover the filling of the Spirit, and restoration to the fellowship [with God the Father] that was broken by that sin.[37]

So, on the cross, the debt of sin owed was paid, and the record of it was erased forever. In time, the forgiveness of sins has to do with restoring fellowship with God the Father and recovering the filling of the Spirit. Do you get it?

You might say, I don't agree. Where does it say that all sins were forgiven at the cross? I think Ephesians 1:7 clearly delineates this. However, if you're still not convinced, then let's attempt to provide further evidence of such by answering the following question.

What about the forgiveness of sins concerning those who are unsaved?
Let's turn in our Bibles to the book of Colossians.

> *Colossians 2:13 And you, being dead in your sins and the uncircumcision of your flesh, hath he quickened together with him, having forgiven you all trespasses;*

If you read this verse without Greek glasses on, it would say something like this: And you, the believers at Colosse, who before you were saved, were spiritually *dead in your sins* (the sin nature) *of your flesh* (body), of which *uncircumcision* is a sign. However, when you responded to the gospel, *he* (God the Holy Spirit) has *quickened* (made you alive) *together with him* (Christ), *having forgiven you* (wiped away) *all trespasses* (all deviations from the truth).

I think you'd agree with me when I say that this appears to be saying that when you were made alive with Christ following your conversion, all of your sins were forgiven. Some would even go so far as to say that the forgiveness of sins occurred at the time when a person was subsequently baptized in water (Acts 2:38). However, what we'll soon find out is that the correct interpretation of this verse will nullify each of these conjectures. Are you ready to find out why?

As I said initially, you need to have Greek glasses on in order to understand what is meant by the phrase *having forgiven*. The Koine Greek will once again help us in this regard. The phrase *having forgiven* are denoted as being in the form of an aorist middle participle. When a verb is designated in the aorist tense with the description of being a participle, this tells that the action of the minor verb, i.e., *having forgiven* precedes the action of the main verb, i.e., *quickened*. As you can see, translating any verse according to the English structure wouldn't yield this unique relationship.

So, what this tells us is that all of the sins of the Corinthian believers were forgiven at a point in time before they were made anew, i.e., when they were unbelievers. The only place prior to salvation where all of their sins were already forgiven was at the cross. *Therefore, the perspective that not all sins were forgiven at the cross isn't accurate.*

•Chastisement

Some believe that chastisement (discipline) from God the Father has only to do with punishment for the committing of certain sins. And that if a believer continually commits certain ones, then the ultimate consequence is the loss of salvation. Is this indeed the case? Let's let Scripture reveal to us what God's purpose is in implementing correction. Please turn to the book of Hebrews.

> *Hebrews 12:11 Now no chastening for the present seemeth to be joyous, but grievous: nevertheless afterward it yieldeth the peaceable fruit of righteousness unto them which are exercised thereby.*

This Scripture conveys to us that *no chastening* (discipline) *seemeth* (appears) *to be joyous* (pleasant), *but grievous* (painful); *nevertheless, afterward* (in the end; in the future) *it yieldeth* (produces something in us if we allow it to). What is it God desires that correction will produce in us? That it hopefully will produce the *peaceable fruit of righteousness* in our lives. What is this all about?

This is otherwise known as actual *righteousness* in ourselves,[38] i.e., peace, calmness, submission in the soul,[39] those fruits by which we gain much, and through which [we're] made happy.[40] The effect is seen in a pure [life] and in a more entire devotedness to God.[41] Oh my God! But wait, this is conditional, right?

In other words, what takes place in our lives only gets produced within us as the Word says *unto them which are exercised thereby.* This means when discipline comes, we, just like someone in the ancient athletic games trained for a contest, so we must exercise ourselves in spiritual matters,[42] such as naming and citing our sins, putting off the old man and putting on the new man, etc. And furthermore, this is also an exercise to give [experience] and make the spiritual combatant victorious.[43]

So, what have we learned concerning chastisement? *We found out that correction concerning the sinful decisions we've made and not confessed to God the Father might involve the implementation of uncomfortable consequences by Him but not toward us as a criminal who has no way out, but for us as His sons and daughters for our spiritual recovery.*

- Salvation and sanctification

There are those who believe that a believer's walk with God will affect their salvation. As verified in the last chapter, salvation is a once and for all event with present continuing results. Sanctification is a daily process that involves recognizing and confessing sinful thoughts, words, and actions and choosing whether to apply God's prescription of His Word. *While sanctification will not impact a believer's standing with God, it will surely reveal whether they're walking in the Spirit or walking in the flesh.*

- Scripture interpretation

Those who believe that the Spirit can leave a believer because of habitual sin, or who believe that not all sins were forgiven at the cross, or who believe that chastisement is punishment for sin with severe consequences, or who believe that sanctification affects salvation, then most likely they'll support the view that salvation can be lost because of habitual sin. And if that's so, then the following verses presented will be interpreted by them in order to justify any of these perceptions. However, following this rendering, we'll analyze the same verse or verses according to the view that salvation cannot be lost due to habitual sin. But before we do, let's attempt to answer this question.

Did you know that in most instances, there are at least three reasons why there's such disparity concerning any doctrinal view?

The first has to do with the method used in interpreting a verse of Scripture. If proper hermeneutics (exegesis) is applied, then the true meaning will have a better chance of being found. What is hermeneutics? Hermeneutics has to do with scriptural interpretation based on an analysis of the grammatical features of the original languages of Hebrew, Aramaic, and Koine Greek, along with the historical background (context).

The second reason has to do with whether the person interpreting a verse or verses is dispensational or non-dispensational in their approach. The dispensationalist is aware that God employs a unique plan for different people living at different times under different biblical covenants for salvation and sanctification. And whatever the protocol for salvation and salvation is for a particular era, only verses from such will be used to verify it. On the other hand, the non-dispensationalist could interpret a verse or verses from other dispensations and apply their meanings to a different dispensation with respect to sanctification and salvation, thus distorting their translation.

And the third one has to do with comparing Scripture with Scripture. What we shouldn't be doing is use only one verse to establish any doctrinal view. In most cases, there should be other verses contained in the writings of a particular dispensation that can clarify and substantiate what we believe is the correct interpretation of a particular biblical passage.

With that said, let's take a look at some verses that are interpreted to indicate that salvation can be lost, and likewise, reinterpreting them again, supporting the view that salvation can't be lost. We'll begin by analyzing verses from the book of Galatians.

Salvation Can Be Lost Because of Habitual Sin

Galatians 5:1-4

> *Stand fast therefore in the liberty wherewith Christ hath made us free, and be not entangled again with the yoke of bondage. Behold, I Paul say unto you, that if ye be circumcised, Christ shall profit you nothing. For I testify again to every man that is circumcised, that he is a debtor to do the whole law. Christ is become of no effect unto you, whosoever of you are justified by the law; ye are fallen from grace.*

The Apostle Paul was instructing the saints at Galatia, saying that whosoever you are that adheres to the admonition that *you are justified* (made righteous) by obeying the commands of *the law*, then you *are fallen from grace*. The phrase *fallen from grace* are interpreted to mean fall out of grace or lose one's salvation because of consistently committing sins that are contrary to that which is delineated according to the Mosaic Law.

Salvation Cannot Be Lost Due to Habitual Sin
The Apostle Paul wasn't speaking about the Galatians' believers'

standing but their spiritual lives, i.e., their walk with God. The phrase *fallen from grace* is the idea that these Christians by putting themselves under the law have put themselves in a place where they have ceased to be in that relation to Christ where they could derive the spiritual benefits from Him which would enable them to live a life pleasing to Him, namely, through the ministry of the Holy Spirit. Thus, Christ [had] no more effect upon them in the living of their Christian lives.[44] Another way of saying this is that Christians had lost their hold upon the grace for daily [living,] which heretofore had been ministered to them by the Holy Spirit.[45] Thus, the phrase *fallen from grace* means not depending on the grace that teaches us about denying ungodliness and worldly lusts (Titus 2:12).

The next group of verses that we'll take a look at is taken from the book of John. Please turn there in your Bibles.

Salvation Can Be Lost Because of Habitual Sin

John 15:1-2

> *I am the true vine, and my Father is the husbandman. Every branch in me that beareth not fruit he taketh away: and every branch that beareth fruit, he purgeth it, that it may bring forth more fruit.*

Every believer in Christ that continually bears no *fruit*, and thus lives in continual sin, will be *taken away*. *Taken away* interprets every branch which has been in Him by true faith - such as have given way to iniquity and made shipwreck of their faith and of their good conscience: all these he taketh away,[46] i.e., they have lost their salvation.

Salvation Cannot Be Lost Due to Habitual Sin

Every believer who is *in me* (attached to Christ) and bears no *fruit*, thus living in continual sin, will be *taken away* which can also be interpreted to mean lift up. With that said, we can reinterpret this part of the verse and say that those Christians who bear no fruit will learn how to do so through the teachings of the four-fold leadership (Ephesians 4:11-12) and ministry of the Holy Spirit (1 John 2:27) in respect to who they are in Christ and how to be conformed to His image.

The next verse that we'll take a look at is found in the book of 2 Peter.

Salvation Can Be Lost Because of Habitual Sin

2 Peter 3:16

> *As also in all his epistles, speaking in them of these things; in which are some things hard to be understood, which they that are unlearned and unstable wrest, as they do also the other scriptures, unto their own destruction.*

In 2 Peter 3:3, the Apostle Peter talked about people who were *scoffers*. They were unbelievers who disregarded the predictions about the second coming or return of the Lord Jesus and the truths about the end of the world. After this, he mentioned that there are doctrines in the epistles of the Apostle Paul that were *hard to be understood* (not easy to be comprehended). And that there were those who are *unlearned* (uninstructed; of people who [haven't] received sufficient instruction in the interpretation of [Scripture][47]) and *unstable* (prone to error) that *wrest* (the act of distorting or misinterpreting the Scriptures through faulty methods of interpretation[48]), which some infer will cause them to live an ungodly sinful life. Subsequently, this would result in their own *destruction* ([consisting of] the loss of eternal life, eternal misery, perdition, [and] the lot of those excluded from the kingdom of God).[49]

Salvation Cannot Be Lost Due to Habitual Sin

Before we attempt to determine what the word *destruction* means, we need to know just who *they* are who are the *unlearned and unstable*. Are they unbelievers? Probably not. Why not? Because if they were, it wouldn't matter whether they were instructed in the interpretation of Scripture because salvation isn't based on this but on repenting of one's sins and believing in Christ. Therefore, what we can deduce is that *they* are believers.

If this is the case, then is there another way to interpret the word *destruction*? Yes, there is. What else could it mean? It can also, in Koine Greek, mean ruin. Is there a way to substantiate this meaning? Yes, there is. It's found in the next verse.

2 Peter 3:17

> *Ye therefore, beloved, seeing ye know these things before, beware lest ye also, being led away with the error of the wicked, fall from your own stedfastness.*

Here, the Apostle Peter was talking to a group of believers whom he called *beloved*. As we'll see, I believe this connotation pertains to their walk with God. He points out to them that what he just said was made known to them at an earlier time. He reminds them to *beware* (be alert; take extra precaution) so that they're also not *led away* (seduced; lured) by *wicked* men (lawless; those who want to sweep large groups of people away from the correct doctrine of Christ[50]). And if this were to be the case, he told them what the result would be, i.e., they would *fall* (be separated) from their *own stedfastness*, i.e., from being "established in the present truth" (2 Peter 1:12)]. Therefore, the stability of the Christian comes from his faith in the Word of God, his knowledge of that Word, and his ability to use that Word in the practical decisions of life.[51]

This question remains. Does it seem unlikely that one group of Christians who were unlearned and ignorant would lose their salvation while another group of Christians who were seemingly more mature but who likewise went astray would not also lose their salvation? Therefore, by comparing Scripture with Scripture, the scriptural conclusion is that those who are unlearned and ignorant would fall into spiritual ruin if they engaged in committing habitual sin. Simply put, they wouldn't grow spiritually and walk in newness of life. While they wouldn't lose their salvation, their life wouldn't evidence the fruit of the Holy Spirit.

In order to hammer home the contrast of scriptural interpretation in respect to salvation, let's take a final look at another group of Scriptures. Please turn to the book of 2 Peter.

Salvation Can Be Lost Because of Habitual Sin

Suggested Reading: 2 Peter 2:1-22

> *1 But there were false prophets also among the people, even as there shall be false teachers among you, who privily shall bring in damnable heresies, even denying the Lord that bought them, and bring upon themselves swift destruction.*

The Apostle Peter was instructing the Christian Jews to watch out, because there would be *false prophets* and *teachers, who privily* (privately; the metaphor is that of a spy or traitor; the introduction of false teaching alongside the true[52]) *shall bring in damnable heresies* (self-chosen doctrines) and deny (denounce) Jesus (they held doctrines which were in denial of the Lord), who *bought them* (Jesus' blood is the ransom paid to divine justice for the debt of sin).

Before we continue, is there any way to determine whether these imposters were Christians? We're told that Christ bought them. What Scripture conveys to us is that everyone, past, present, or future, was bought by Christ (1 John 2:2). I think the key word that will help us in this determination is *denying*.

Another way to describe this word is to say that this disavowal seems to have consisted of an inadequate view of the Person and Work of Christ, and their relation to the problem of human sin.[53] The consequence of such was that *they will bring upon themselves swift* (impending) *destruction* (eternal destruction). It appears that Scripture supports the view that these prophets and teachers were unbelievers.

Furthermore, the apostle informs us that some believers had already decided to follow their teachings. If this were indeed the case, and it is, then here's what he had to say about what was contained in the messages that drew them in.

> *18 For when they speak great swelling words of vanity, they allure through the lusts of the flesh, through much wantonness, those that were clean escaped from them who live in error.*

When *those* (Christians) that *were clean escaped* (those who are in the early stage of their escape) *from them who live in error* (wrong [opinions] relative to morals or religion[54]), heard *great swelling* (pretentious; sounding impressive) *words of vanity* (devoid of truth), they were allured (enticed; deceived) by teachings that promoted the *lusts* (desires) *of the flesh*, which included immoral sexual acts that are presented as legitimate expressions of Christian freedom.

> *20 For if after they have escaped the pollutions of the world through the knowledge of the Lord and Saviour Jesus Christ, they are again entangled therein, and overcome, the latter end is worse with them than the beginning.*

Then, the Apostle Peter goes on to say what impact this will have in their life. *For if after they* (those whom converted to the Christian faith) *have escaped* (the moral and ethical [influences] of the Word of God had acted as [a deterrent][55]) *the pollutions* (licentious passions of the flesh[56]) *of the world through the knowledge* (of one that truly knows Christ, who has been taught by him to put off the old man and to put on the new man[57]) *of the Lord and Savior Jesus Christ, and are again entangled* (as they persisted in the false teaching that grace gave license to sin) *therein* to their former immoral lives, *and are overcome* (trapped again by the powers of these worldly lusts[58]), then *the latter end* (the current state they're in) *is worse* experientially (because when they found the answers to address their eternal state and help them overcome the weaknesses of their flesh, they chose to go back to living their life that offers no solutions. And along with this, they also became a witness to others that they're no longer under the restraints by which they had professedly bound themselves[59]) *than the beginning* (of their new life in Christ).

> *21 For it had been better for them not to have known the way of righteousness, than, after they have known it, to turn from the holy commandment delivered unto them.*

It had been better for them not to have known the way of righteousness (a life lived according to the will of God[60]) than to *have* fully *known* about *it* and *turn from* (be unfaithful to) *the holy commandment* (the gospel; Christian teaching as a whole) in which they were instructed.

There are two ideas to be considered here. The first is what is meant by the statement that it *had been better for them not to have known the way of righteousness*. Some might say that what is being implied is that it would have been better if they hadn't been saved in the first place. This rendering would negate God's desire for all men to be saved and come to the knowledge of the truth (1 Timothy 2:3-4). My personal opinion is that what is being expressed here is the sentiment that the life they're now evidencing dishonors before others the new way of life they used to follow. It discredits it.

The second has to do with their eternal state. Under this view, the phrase *turn from the holy commandment* means that they have fallen away from the gospel, i.e., they've lost their salvation.

Salvation Cannot Be Lost Due to Habitual Sin

Did they lose their salvation? A couple of verses later in 2 Peter chapter 2, we're told what the consequences are for any believer if they choose to live according to the lusts of their flesh.

> *22 But it is happened unto them according to the true proverb, The dog is turned to his own vomit again; and the sow that was washed to her wallowing in the mire.*

Like the offensive habits of a dog that will eat their own vomit, so does a believer who has decided to abandon the way of righteousness. They had vomited their former way of life at salvation and have determined to be committed to that which they detested. This has to do with their walk with God and not their standing (salvation).

We have one more Scripture to look at from the book of 1 John. However, this one won't have to do with a believer losing their salvation. *But rather, what it has to do with is the perspective that if someone is committing habitual sin, then this reveals that they weren't saved in the first place.* This Scripture is probably the primary one which those who believe this premise use to support it.

A Believer Can't Commit Habitual Sin

1 John 3:9

> *Whosoever is born of God doth not commit sin; for his seed remaineth in him: and he cannot sin, because he is born of God.*

This is a fascinating verse pertaining to the chronic committing of sin by a Christian. It says that *whosoever is born of God* (has been made the recipient of divine life[61]) won't continually choose to sin as they formally did because God's *seed* (divine life) *remaineth* (abides) *in him.* Therefore, *he cannot* continually *commit sin* because *he is born of God.* It can be deduced that if someone professes to be a Christian and lives in perpetual sin, then they can't be saved.

Both of the verbs, *doth commit* and *cannot*, in Koine Greek, are in the forms of a present active indicative and present passive indicative, respectively, indicating that what's being emphasized here is the continual committing of sin in the present. Based on the wording of this verse, it does appear that this is what's being said. That someone, who's a believer cannot continue to commit sin and if they do, then they were never saved. However, I think of the adage, never let one verse be used to substantiate a doctrinal view.

A Believer Can Commit Habitual Sin

Whosoever is born of God doth not continually *commit sin; for his seed* (God's divine nature) *remaineth* (abides) *in him.* In order to interpret this correctly, we need to apply Koine Greek.

The verb *born* is in the form of a perfect passive participle. The perfect tense speaks of the completed act of regeneration in the past, at salvation, with present continuing results. In other words, the person who has been made the recipient of divine life [is,] by nature, and that permanently, a spiritually alive individual.[62] Therefore, they cannot commit [sin] because his higher nature, as begotten of God, doth not sin.[63]

This isn't saying that a believer can't habitually sin. They can. However, when they were born again, they became a perfect new creation with a supernatural nature. Therefore, sin can never spring from what a Christian truly is at the level of his regenerate being.[64] Our *who* and our *do* are a million miles apart. Our do cannot affect our who, i.e., the new person we've become. Likewise, there's nothing that can undo our *who* as the following verses testify.

> *Romans 8:38-39 For I am persuaded, that neither death, nor life, nor angels, nor principalities, nor powers, nor things present, nor things to come, Nor height, nor depth, nor any other creature, shall be able to separate us from the love of God, which is in Christ Jesus our Lord.*

I could mention more Scriptures, but I hope what has been studied is enough to assure you that your salvation and the additional blessings associated with it can never be lost due to sin. Furthermore, if you're a Christian and are living in habitual sin, you're still a Christian living in reoccurring sin. And God will be working on your behalf for the purpose of restoration.

Now, it's time to introduce you to all of the blessings you have received at salvation. These will surprise, encourage, and ground you in your new standing in Christ. Are you ready to find out all about them? Let's go.

5

YOU ARE SEALED

I'm sure that you have some idea of what it means when something is sealed. When we send a letter, we make sure that the flap of the envelop is securely glued so that the document inside cannot fall out. We also attach our name and address in the front, indicating who it's from, along with including the name and address of where it's going. Imported or exported goods of any kind are placed in some type of container so that they're protected from damage, along with providing the necessary identification from the seller to the purchaser. Did you know that during the time of Christ, a wax seal would have a mark of ownership or identification stamped in it, identifying who was attesting to what was inside the container that had been sealed?[65] Likewise, were you aware that at salvation, something like this happened to you? Please turn in your Bibles to the book of Ephesians, and we'll find out what this was.

Ephesians 1:13

> *In whom ye also trusted, after that ye heard the word of truth,*

> *the gospel of your salvation: in whom also after that ye*
> *believed, ye were sealed with that holy Spirit of promise,*

When you believed the gospel, you were and are *sealed* with the Holy Spirit! What does it mean when Scripture says that you're sealed? Let's begin by translating this verse. *In whom* (Christ), after you *heard the word of truth*, i.e., *the gospel of your salvation* (the good news that Christ died for [your] sins, was buried, and rose again[66]), you *believed* (acknowledged Him as your savior) and *were sealed with that holy Spirit*.

The phrase *ye were sealed* in Koine Greek is a verb that's in the aorist passive indicative. This tells us that the moment someone believes the gospel, it's certain that they receive the sealing of the Holy Spirit.

And what this seal refers to is the Holy Spirit Himself. "In the symbolism of [Scripture,] a seal signifies (1) A finished transaction ([Jeremiah] 32:9,10; John 17:4; 19:30), (2) Ownership ([Jeremiah] 32:11,12; 2 Timothy 2:19]), [and] (3) Security ([Ester 8:8; Daniel 6:17; Ephesians 4:30])." Thus, God places the Holy Spirit in us permanently … indicating that the great transaction in which God the Son paid for sin, thus satisfying the just demand of God's holy law, is finished; that we saints belong to Him as His heritage, and that [we're] eternally secure.[67]

Did you really grasp what was just said?

Let's restate it. God the Father, by the sealing of the Holy Spirit in a believer's new life, indicates who is His, i.e., you're owned by Him. And He, the Spirit, will never leave you. And wait, there's more.

> *14 Which is the earnest of our inheritance until the*
> *redemption of the purchased possession, unto the praise of*
> *his glory.*

Which (the Spirit) *is the earnest* (the down payment; the "deposit" of the Holy Spirit is a little bit of heaven in believers' lives with a guarantee of much more yet to come;[68] as applied to the Holy Spirit, and his influences on the [heart, it] refers to those influences as a pledge of the future glories which await Christians in heaven[69]) *of our inheritance* (guaranteeing salvation and heaven) until the believer's *redemption* (the completion of such; the deliverance of the creature from the bondage of corruption, and from the usurping prince of this world, into the glorious liberty of the children of God;[70] glorification, the act of God transforming the present bodies of believers into perfect, sinless, deathless bodies.[71]

Just think about what beautiful truths are associated with the sealing of the Holy Spirit. *He comes to indwell you permanently; He's the mark that signifies that God owns you; that you're eternally secure, and your salvation, and future ascension to heaven is guaranteed.* Glory be to God! Shout for joy!

Are you ready to find out another amazing truth about who you are? Let's go.

6

YOU ARE SAVED

Have you ever wished you could be delivered from something that appeared to have no end? Here's an article about such an event.

BLACK DEATH

The Black Death was a devastating global epidemic of bubonic plague that struck Europe and Asia in the mid-1300s. The plague arrived in Europe in October 1347, when [twelve] ships from the Black Sea docked at the Sicilian port of Messina. People gathered on the docks were met with a horrifying surprise: Most sailors aboard the ships were dead, and those still alive were gravely ill and covered in black boils that oozed blood and pus. Sicilian authorities hastily ordered the fleet of "death ships" out of the [harbor. Still,] it was too late: Over the next five years, the Black Death would kill more than [twenty] million people in Europe—almost one-third of the continent's population.

. . .

How Did the Black Plague Start?

Even before the "death ships" pulled into port at Messina, many Europeans had heard rumors about a "Great Pestilence" that was carving a deadly path across the trade routes of the Near and Far East. Indeed, in the early 1340s, the disease had struck China, India, Persia, [Syria,] and Egypt.

The plague is thought to have originated in Asia over 2,000 years ago and was likely spread by trading ships, though recent research has indicated the pathogen responsible for the Black Death may have existed in Europe as early as 3000 B.C.

Symptoms of the Black Plague

Europeans were scarcely equipped for the horrible reality of the Black Death. "In men and women alike," the Italian poet Giovanni Boccaccio wrote, "at the beginning of the malady, certain swellings, either on the groin or under the armpits…waxed to the bigness of a common apple, others to the size of an egg, some more and some less, and these the vulgar named plague-boils."

Blood and pus seeped out of these strange swellings, which were followed by a host of other unpleasant symptoms—fever, chills, vomiting, diarrhea, terrible aches and pains—and then, in short order, death. The Bubonic Plague attacks the lymphatic system, causing swelling in the lymph nodes. If untreated, the infection can spread to the blood or lungs.

How Did the Black Death Spread?

The Black Death was terrifyingly, indiscriminately contagious: "the mere touching of the clothes," wrote Boccaccio, "appeared to itself to communicate the malady to the toucher." The disease was also terrifyingly efficient. People who were perfectly healthy when they went to bed at night could be dead by morning.

. . .

Understanding the Black Death

Today, scientists understand that the Black Death, now known as the plague, [was] spread by a bacillus called *Yersinia pestis*. (The French biologist Alexandre Yersin discovered this germ at the end of the 19th century.) They know that the bacillus travels from person to person through the air, as well as through the bite of infected fleas and rats. Both of these pests could be found almost everywhere in medieval Europe, but they were particularly at home aboard ships of all kinds—which is how the deadly plague made its way through one European port city after another.

Not long after it struck Messina, the Black Death spread to the port of Marseilles in France and the port of Tunis in North Africa. Then it reached Rome and Florence, two cities at the center of an elaborate web of trade routes. By the middle of 1348, the Black Death had struck Paris, Bordeaux, [Lyon,] and London.

Today, this grim sequence of events is terrifying but comprehensible. In the middle of the 14th century, however, there seemed to be no rational explanation for it. No one knew exactly how the Black Death was transmitted from one patient to another, and no one knew how to prevent or treat it. According to one doctor, for example, "instantaneous death occurs when the aerial spirit escaping from the eyes of the sick man strikes the healthy person standing near and looking at the sick."

How Do You Treat the Black Death?

Physicians relied on crude and unsophisticated techniques such as bloodletting and boil-lancing (practices that were dangerous as well as unsanitary) and superstitious practices such as burning aromatic herbs and bathing in rosewater or vinegar. Meanwhile, in a panic, healthy people did all they could to avoid the sick. Doctors refused to see [patients,] priests refused to administer last [rites,] and shopkeepers closed their stores. Many people fled the cities for the countryside, but even [there,] they could not escape the disease: It affected cows, sheep, goats, [pigs,] and chickens as well as people.

In fact, so many sheep died that one of the consequences of the Black Death was a European wool shortage. And many people, desperate to save themselves, even abandoned their sick and dying loved ones. "Thus doing," Boccaccio wrote, "each thought to secure immunity for himself."

Black Plague: God's Punishment?

Because they [didn't] understand the biology of the disease, many people believed that the Black Death was a kind of divine punishment —retribution for sins against God such as greed, blasphemy, heresy, [fornication,] and worldliness.

By this logic, the only way to overcome the plague was to win God's forgiveness. Some people believed that the way to do this was to purge their communities of heretics and other troublemakers—so, for example, many thousands of Jews were massacred in 1348 and 1349. (Thousands more fled to the sparsely populated regions of Eastern Europe, where they could be relatively safe from the rampaging mobs in the cities.)

Some people coped with the terror and uncertainty of the Black Death epidemic by lashing out at their neighbors; others coped by turning inward and fretting about the condition of their own souls.

Flagellants

Some upper-class men joined processions of flagellants that traveled from town to town and engaged in public displays of penance and punishment: They would beat themselves and one another with heavy leather straps studded with sharp pieces of metal while the townspeople looked on. For [thirty-three and a half] days, the flagellants repeated this ritual three times a day. Then they would move on to the next town and begin the process over again.

Though the flagellant movement did provide some comfort to people who felt powerless in the face of inexplicable tragedy, it soon began to worry the [pope], whose authority the flagellants had begun to usurp. In the face of this papal resistance, the movement disintegrated.

How Did the Black Death End?

The plague never really [ended,] and it returned with a vengeance years later. But officials in the port city of Ragusa were able to slow its spread by keeping arriving sailors in isolation until it was clear they were not carrying the disease—creating social distancing that relied on isolation to slow the spread of the disease.

The sailors were initially held on their ships for [thirty] days (a [*Trentino*]), a period that was later increased to [forty] days, or a *quarantine*—the origin of the term "quarantine" and a practice still used today.

Does the Black Plague Still Exist?

The Black Death epidemic had run its course by the early 1350s, but the plague reappeared every few generations for centuries. Modern sanitation and [public health] practices have greatly mitigated the impact of the disease but have not eliminated it. While antibiotics are available to treat the Black Death, according to The World Health Organization, there are still [one thousand to three thousand] cases of plague every year.[72]

Did you know that there's a death, believe it or not, that never ends? What it's called and how someone who has it can be cured is found in the book of Ephesians. Please turn there in your Bibles.

Ephesians 2:8

> *For by grace are ye saved through faith; and that not of yourselves: it is the gift of God:*

By grace (the source of salvation which proceeds from that particular gracious act of God the Son in dying upon the Cross to pay man's penalty incurred by him through sin[73]) *are ye saved* (deliverance from a present spiritual death[74]) *through faith* (accepting grace; believing the gospel).

The verb *saved* in Koine Greek is in the form of a perfect passive participle. What we can conclude is that these believers received the reality of being saved because they accepted grace at a point of time in the past with present continual results, i.e., they remain in a perpetual saved state.

What we've learned is that faith not the work of an individual but an acceptance of what's presented. And once you're saved, you're saved forever from living a life that has no connection to God. Saved forever from living a life dependent on self and saved from not knowing what life is truly about. And ultimately saved from eternal spiritual death.

So, what's the cure for being rescued from current and future eternal spiritual death? It's by accepting the gospel of Christ. If someone responds favorably to this good news, it's said that they become spiritually alive now and evermore. The God that exists in the person of the Holy Spirit comes to live inside of them, providing a new nature, a new direction, that is, a spiritual one, and a new purpose. This is a purpose guided by the true meaning of life, i.e., to get to know God personally, to become like Him, thus finding true inner happiness and sharing about such wherever you go.

What we'll talk about next is the fact that you have more than two parents. Huh? How can this be? What we'll learn about the upcoming blessing will provide us with clarity about this new spiritual reality.

7

YOU ARE A CHILD OF GOD

*D*id you know that in certain states in America, a parent has no legal obligation to provide an inheritance for any of their children after they die? If they have a reason, or no reason at all, as long as the will testifies of this, then a child or children can be denied. Here's another interesting tidbit about inheritance.

What if there's more owed than what remains of the assets? Can the beneficiaries take the equity and not be responsible for paying off the debts? No, the debts must be paid off first.

If the heirs are children (under 18 years of age), they're not responsible for a deceased parent's debt. Did you know that in certain parts of the world, children can be held responsible for paying back the loans of their parents. When this happens, what transpires is what's called bonded labor. Let's take a further look at what this is all about.

WHAT IS BONDED [LABOR]?
"We [don't stop even if we're] ill – what if our debt is increasing? So, we don't dare to stop. "[Other workers] tried to leave, but two got

caught. They locked them up and started beating them. They told the workers, 'If you want to go from here, you must pay [sixty-thousand] that is your debt.'"

Puspal, [a] former brick kiln worker in Punjab, India

Puspal is one of [the] millions of people worldwide exploited through debt bondage (also called debt slavery), which occurs when a person is forced to work to pay off a debt.

According to [estimates,] in 2022, around one-fifth of all people in forced [labor] exploitation in the private economy are in situations of debt bondage. Thankfully, Puspal managed to leave her employer thanks to the support her family received from our project partners. However, not every victim of bonded [labor] is able to leave – many live in fear of violence or of passing their debt on to their children.

People who experience debt bondage have often been tricked into working for little or no pay. In many [cases,] [they're] forced to pay off extortionate fees associated with their recruitment, [accommodation,] or food, with no control over the debt they have accrued. Most or all of the money they earn goes to pay off their ["loan."]

In many cases, people who experience debt bondage work far more, and for far longer, than it should take to pay off their loans, working tirelessly without seeing an end to their debt. Recent data shows that the initial months of the Covid-19 pandemic resulted in a rise in reports of debt bondage, as many workers were unable to borrow money through formal channels.

Bonded [labor] has existed for hundreds of years. After the Transatlantic slave trade was abolished in the 1800s, many formerly enslaved people were forced into indentured [labor] – a form of debt bondage – for many years on plantations in Africa, the [Caribbean,] and South-East Asia.

Today, bonded [labor] is most widespread in South Asian [countries,] including India and Pakistan, where it flourishes, for example, in agriculture, brick kilns, mills, [mines,] and factories. It often occurs alongside other forms of modern [slavery,] such as human trafficking. *In some societies, debt is shared by whole families who have to work to pay off debts taken on by a relative. Sometimes, the debt can even be inherited by children, who are then held in slavery because of a loan their parents took out decades ago.*

In the private sector, unscrupulous [labor] brokers and recruitment agencies can trap people in debt bondage. Some charge steep recruitment fees to workers, which can include payment to secure a job or to pay for training and insurance. These fees can lead to debt bondage, leaving workers toiling for little or no pay until the debt is repaid. Migrant workers are particularly vulnerable to this form of exploitation, for [example, if they're] dependent on recruiting agencies.

Many people in debt bondage have their passports and other ID documents seized by their employers, leaving the workers unable to leave [or living] in fear of being [criminalized]. Some victims of debt bondage face threats, [intimidation,] and violence from the people that exploit them.

Although bonded [labor] is illegal, laws against it are rarely enforced, particularly in cases where people in power benefit directly from exploiting others. Like many forms of modern slavery, bonded [labor flourishes where corruption, poverty,] and discrimination are common. Limited access to justice, [education,] and jobs for discriminated groups make it difficult for them to get out of poverty.[75]

Did you know that there are no constraints on your inheritance in Christ? The book of Galatians provides us with clarity on this declaration.

Galatians 3:26-27

For ye are all the children of God by faith in Christ Jesus.

Under the Mosaic Law, until a son arrived at age, he was in many respects not different from a servant. He was under laws and restraints; and subject to the will of another. When of age, he entered on the privileges of heirship, and was free to act for himself[76] (Galatians 4:1-2). However, when someone responds to the gospel, they become a child of God, of full age, who's free from the law and automatically admitted to the benefits of the sons and daughters of God. The phrase *children of God* denote those who've come into the full enjoyment, so far as the present life is concerned, of the position [which their new] birth had entitled them to.[77]

So, if someone were to ask you to describe yourself in respect to your new faith, you'd say, I'm a child of God who's been declared an adult to enjoy all the privileges and rights of my inheritance as a son or daughter of God with all debts paid for by Christ's death on the cross.

And because of such, the next blessing tells you what you're called now that you've been admitted to the full rights of the family of God.

8

YOU ARE AN HEIR

*I*n the world we live in, this can be a very contentious issue. In my teenage years, there was a period of time when I lived with my mom and dad next door to my Italian grandparents. At times, I'd go over to their house for lunch. Usually, my grandmother always had something cooking. My favorite dish was rice and butter. Yes, that's right.

Being Italian, she was a very good cook. She usually also had some sort of pasta dish prepared. When offered, I'd always accept. On one particular day, my grandfather asked me if I'd like to play an Italian card game called Briscola. To which I said yes. So, he taught me how to play this game of cards that he learned when he lived as a little boy in Italy. From there on out, my grandfather and I would eat and play cards whenever I visited for lunch.

One day, unexpectedly, he told to me that he'd like to give me his car when I was old enough to drive. This was a 1967 Dodge Dart that had slightly over [ten thousand] miles on it. He maintained it so rigorously that you'd have thought it was a new car. Finally, the time came when I turned sixteen, and subsequently took driving lessons and passed the road test, which my father conveyed to him.

This caused quite a stir amongst my father's brother and five sisters. My dad told me that all his siblings were going to meet at my grandfather's house to discuss this situation. I thought it was a done deal. Why wouldn't my aunts and uncles not want me to have this car? I was frequently reminded by both my grandfather and grandmother that carrying the Rondinone name was of primary importance to them. And at that time, I was the only male grandson who was carrying their last name. So, I thought this carried some influence as to the outcome.

While I waited at home with anticipation and excitement about receiving the news that I'd be getting this car, my father finally arrived home. When he called me to discuss what had transpired, I could immediately see on his face that this meeting didn't go well. He told me that, unfortunately, one of my younger cousins, who was about to enter his first year of college, got the car. I was devastated. What really hurt the most was the knowledge that I'd been told by my grandfather that this was going to be my car at the appropriate time. And somehow, his promise was altered by his sons and daughters, i.e., my aunts and uncles, whom I'd always looked up to.

Have you ever been disappointed being an heir who didn't receive what they were promised at said time? Well, did you know that you are an heir, an heir of God, being witnessed of such by the Holy Spirit, who's guaranteed what God has promised you? Let's find out more about how the Spirit gives us witness and what it is that you're assured of receiving at salvation. The book of Romans will tell us more about this.

Romans 8:16-17

> *The Spirit itself beareth witness with our spirit, that we are the children of God: And if children, then heirs; heirs of God, and joint-heirs with Christ; if so be that we suffer with him, that we may be also glorified together.*

As a child of God, the Holy Spirit has given you *witness* (evidence) of His presence *with* your *spirit* (human spirit; mind) in a joint testimony to the fact that [you're] a child of God[78] by producing in [you] the appropriate effects of His influence. And because you are God's child, you're also an heir like your fellow believers who are *heirs; heirs* (recipients of all spiritual blessings now[79]) *of God, and joint-heirs with Christ* (and in the future [you'll] share with the Lord Jesus in all the riches of God's kingdom[80]). Over time, these blessings that you've been given will be evidenced to yourself and others as you grow spiritually.

So, to be an heir means that at salvation you were the recipient of all spiritual blessings, and still are, and will continue to be.

The blessing that we'll take a look at next talks about the fact that you've been put right with God. Any guess what word describes this spiritual reality?

9

YOU ARE JUSTIFIED

For many years, there was a medical condition that generated such fear and alarm in society that many who were diagnosed with it were transported to isolated areas and *never heard from again*. Any idea what infectious disease I'm referring to? Some of those that had it were recorded in Scripture as having come to Jesus for healing (Matthew 8:2). I've provided an article for us to read that discusses what caused this, whether people are still becoming infected with it and what has been done to prevent it.

SURVIVING LEPROSY: A STORY OF GRACE
 Written by MAP Staff | January 30, 2018 at 3:06 PM
 Sunday was World Leprosy Day, a day that aims to raise awareness of a disease that many people believe to be extinct. The global elimination of leprosy ([i.e.,] a prevalence rate of less than [one case per ten thousand people at the global level) was officially announced in 2000. In reality, approximately [two hundred ten thousand new cases are diagnosed each year,] and some believe millions more are living undiagnosed.

Leprosy is a chronic, infectious disease that develops slowly, with an average incubation period of five years. It is caused by a bacterium, Mycobacterium leprae, and chiefly affects the skin, peripheral nerves, mucous membranes of the respiratory tract, and eyes. [It's curable. But when left untreated,] they can cause severe deformities and have [life-threatening] consequences.

Multidrug therapy treatments have been provided worldwide by the WHO free of charge since 1995. [It's] a simple yet highly effective cure for all types of leprosy. Sadly, however, those living with the disease are still often stigmatized and shunned from their communities.

MAP International [has been] engaged in the fight to end leprosy in West Africa since early 2002. We joined with renowned partners American Leprosy Missions, Effect: Hope and The Leprosy Mission Ireland. The fight against leprosy included strategies focused on cure, [care,] and ending the disease.

In addition to teaching awareness, [prevention,] and treatment of these diseases to the local community, MAP also trained healthcare professionals to identify symptoms and begin treatment in the earliest stages of the disease to save lives.

[Here's] one story of survival that MAP shared nearly two years ago. [It's a story as touching today as it was then. It's a story about a woman named] Grace.

Suffering from leprosy [hasn't been easy. Early on, no one knew why, as a young child,] Grace had scaly patches on her hands. Leprosy, although curable, carries a stigma that causes people, even young [children,] to be alienated from their community. Grace is tough, she's twelve years old and has been suffering from leprosy since she was three years old. [She's] the only daughter living with six brothers in rural Cote d'Ivoire.

Seeking a normal life for her daughter, Grace's mother sent her to Chinese healers in the [community,] and for a short time - it worked. When the same patches reappeared on her hands, her mother traveled to a rural clinic where MAP International and American Leprosy Missions worked to prevent the spread of leprosy.

"The nurse gave me some injections, and a few days [later, my hands were back to normal," said Grace.]

The following year her leprosy came back, and Grace knew just where to go – the clinic. She received a full course of treatment and her patches once again cleared. As her mother shared after her treatment:

"[I'd] like to say thank you to God today for showing me the right way to treat my daughter for leprosy. She has suffered from this since she was three. I tried so many different treatments, but the disease [wouldn't stop. I didn't know my daughter had leprosy,] and it's a bad disease that can deform [people;] it could have deformed my daughter.

God did a miracle by showing me the best way to treat her today. My daughter [won't] have a deformity because of the nurse that treated her. Thank you, [God, again." Grace's mother, Odette.][81]

Did you know that like someone who has had leprosy and was either shunned or alienated, every person born into this world is condemned? Why is this the case? Please turn to the book of Romans and find out.

Romans 5:12

> *Wherefore, as by one man sin entered into the world, and death by sin; and so death passed upon all men, for that all have sinned:*

God placed the first man, Adam, and his wife, Eve, to live in a perfect environment without sin. They were instructed that every fruit bearing tree was good to eat from except one called the tree of the knowledge of good and evil. Through deception and coercion by a serpent, i.e., the Devil, each of them partook of this forbidden fruit and thus sinned. Because of this disobedience or transgression, man's nature was corrupted.

Some call this the sin nature, which is passed down from the father, when his sperm (reproductive cells) joins with the female egg and the child's body begins to form. It's believed that this nature is found in the blood.

Thereby, *sin* (the sin nature) *entered* (was transmitted) *into the world* (Adam's descendants), and *death* (physical and spiritual death – Romans 6:23) *passed upon* (spread throughout) *all men*. Thus, each person in their depraved state is considered as a vessel of wrath alienated from God (Romans 9:22). Fortunately, like the medicine that Grace took for her leprosy, there's available for each of us a cure out from the fallen state that's found in the same book of Romans.

Romans 5:1

Therefore being justified by faith, we have peace with God through our Lord Jesus Christ:

You're *justified* (declared righteous; put right with God; the passing out of the condemned condition into an assurance of God's love;[82] guiltless and uncondemned and righteous in a righteousness which God accepts, the Lord Jesus[83]) *by faith* ([belief] in a [Savior] who died for us and rose again[84]), and because of such you *have peace with God* the Father (entered into a state of peace; the state of reconciliation; the result of a legal standing; always on God's side; no longer the object of God's displeasure[85]) *through our Lord Jesus Christ* (because we're accepted in Him).

And unlike Grace, you don't have to take medicine again. *You're justified. You've entered into an assurance of God's love, having passed out of a condemned condition always being on God's side.* Take a hold of that in your mind and never let it go.

The next spiritual reality that has taken place in our lives is one that we have a difficult time believing because when we think about what's being said about us, we tend to look at our shortcomings and believe this can't be so.

10

YOU ARE SANCTIFIED

Have you ever thought of calling someone holy? Usually, this refers to a person involved with a particular faith that's performing good works for the less fortunate. In some religious circles, when someone is considered holy, they're designated as a saint. In one particular faith, Catholicism, this classification isn't taken lightly. There are a few stages, four to be exact, that must be followed for someone to be considered as such. Are you aware of what each of these levels are about? I'm certainly not. The following article will unveil to us what these consist of.

WHO BECOMES A SAINT IN THE CATHOLIC CHURCH, AND IS THAT CHANGING?

Any Catholic or group of Catholics can request that the bishop open a case. [They'll] need to name a formal intermediary, called the "postulator," [who'll] promote the cause of the saint. At this point, the candidate is called "a servant of God."

A formal investigation examines [the] "servant of God's" life. Those who knew the candidate are interviewed, and affidavits for and against the candidate are reviewed. Also, the candidate's writings – if any exist – are examined for consistency with Catholic doctrine. A "promoter of justice" named by the local bishop ensures that proper procedures are [followed,] and a notary certifies the documentation.

The proceedings of the investigation, called "Acta" or "The Acts," are forwarded to the Congregation for the Causes of the Saints in Rome. The Congregation for the Causes of the Saints is large, with a prefect, a secretary, [an undersecretary, and a staff of twenty-three people. There are also over thirty] cardinals and bishops associated with the congregation's work at various stages.

The Congregation for the Causes of the Saints appoints a "relator" (one of five who currently work for the congregation) who supervises the postulator in writing a position paper called a "positio." The positio argues for the virtues of the servant of God and can be thousands of pages long. The congregation examines the positio and members vote "yes" or "no" on the cause. "Yes" votes must be unanimous.

The final decision lies with the pope. When he signs a "Decree of Heroic Virtue," the person becomes "venerable." Then two stages remain: beatification and sainthood.[86]

Here's my question for you to consider. Do you think of yourself as a saint, i.e., someone who is holy? And what about God? Do you believe that He considers you as such? Let's find out. If you have your Bible handy, please go to the book of Hebrews.

Hebrews 10:9-10

> *Then said he, Lo, I come to do thy will, O God. He taketh away the first, that he may establish the second. By the which will we are sanctified through the offering of the body of Jesus Christ once for all.*

We're told that Jesus came to do His father's *will*, i.e., to take *away the first* (set aside the legal system of sacrifices that are of no value in removing sin) and *establish the second* (the Divine will, willing our redemption through Christ, and perfectly fulfilled by him[87]). *By which will* you *are sanctified* (have been made holy; from unholy alienation into a state of consecration to God[88]) *through the offering of the body* (the atonement; perfectly holy body) *of Jesus Christ* as a once and for all sacrifice for sin.

What else we can learn about being *sanctified* is that this verb in Koine Greek is in the form of a perfect passive participle. By God's will, during the establishment of the second covenant of grace, the Hebrew believers responded to His invitation of salvation, and received sanctification (the state of holiness) at this moment in time with present continual results, i.e., they remain in a perpetual sanctified state.

In the eyes of God, like them, you're holy and therefore this is how you should see yourself. This isn't based on whether you perform good works or whether your behavior is approved of by God or others. With that said, can you answer this question? Are you a saint?

Don't look at your condition when answering this question. Simply believe in God's declaration about you. *You're holy or are constantly in a state of holiness in the present. And yes, you're a saint.* This will never change in God's eyes and neither should it in yours. And this reality will be worked out in your new life in Christ as you grow spiritually. Hallelujah!

Another declaration about our new lives that we'll look at next is one that I've wrestled with for years. Thank God that He's declared in His Word how we should perceive and address this.

11

YOU ARE PERFECTED

Before I was saved, I made many decisions that were self-centered and, thus, self-destructive. One of them had to do with a relationship that I had with a young lady when I was in my early twenties. I was introduced to her by my best friend's wife.

She came from an Italian family, like me. We went on many dates and simply enjoyed each other's company. One thing led to another, and we got intimate. This became a regular occurrence over many months until one day, I received a phone call from a member of her family letting me know that she was pregnant.

What was a non-committal relationship became a matter of, what should we do next? She wanted to get married, but I was hesitant. I felt that I wasn't ready to make a long-term commitment. This didn't sit well with her and her family. As time went by, a final decision needed to be made.

However, in the midst of it all, I received a phone call from one of her family members letting me know that she had a miscarriage. I was told in no uncertain terms to no longer have anything to do with her again. And so, I never heard from her anymore.

A few years later, I found Christ, or rather He found me. And so, a new life had begun. I began to think, speak, and act differently. After many years had gone by, I decided to start writing and publishing books on various spiritual topics. One of the manuscripts had to do with forgiveness and guilt.

As I was writing it, I asked God if I needed to make amends for any decisions that I'd made in my past. Two names came up. One had to do with a fellow believer, and the other had to do with this girl. I was initially filled with guilt and shame as to how I had mistreated each one of them. So, I proceeded to search for their phone numbers, call them up, admit, apologize for my past misconduct, and clear my conscience.

I was able to get a hold of the fellow believer and address the issue. He accepted my apology. Then, I tried to get in touch with the woman. I did an online search and found many men and women that went by her maiden name. Some of them even lived in the state where she was from. I called as many as possible, but there was no connection to her. So, this attempt ended.

I did what I believed God put on my heart. I followed through the best that I could. My guilt is gone. Thank you, Lord.

What about you? Do you harbor any regrets? Do you believe that God holds you accountable for any of your sins that His Son has paid the penalty for on the cross? Might He put on your heart to address certain ones?

Let's find out how He thinks about you now that you've become His son or daughter. The book of Hebrews is where we'll turn to next.

Hebrews 10:14

> *For by one offering he hath perfected for ever them that are sanctified.*

By Christ's death on the cross, He has *perfected for ever them that are sanctified* (progressive sanctification; those that are being made holy). What does it mean when this verse says that believers are *perfected* forever? *This word means that you have a perfect standing before God by*

Christ's one offering of Himself on the cross which constitutes that your sins were fully taken away and your conscience was cleansed from guilt.

This tells us that on the cross, Christ took your place. He paid the debt or penalty owed for every sin that you have or ever will commit. And along with this, He wiped away the record of every one of your sins, thus removing every ounce of guilt associated with each one.

The verb *perfected* in Koine Greek is in the form a perfect active indicative. In this instance, this verse could be interpreted to say that you, who has believed in the one offering of Christ, were not only sanctified but perfected at the same point in time in the past with the effects of the reality of your sins being forgiven and the guilt removed remain persisting in your new life in the present.

So, why should you no longer carry shame around with you? It's because you're a new creation, i.e., a new person with a unique nature. Stop reminding yourself of what you've done in the past and bring about a resurgence of regret all over again unless the Holy Spirit influences you to make amends with those whom you've hurt.

What we'll talk about next are two things that God has given us that can never be taken away by someone else or something we've done. Are you ready to find out what these are? Then please turn the page.

12

YOU ARE REDEEMED AND FORGIVEN

In life, what we value most can be taken from us unexpectedly. And when a celebrity's very life has abruptly ended, we're often in a state of shock and disbelief. I remember watching a certain martial arts star in an American weekly TV show and later in some action feature films. Here's the brief story about his demise.

HOW DID BRUCE LEE DIE?

With a nickname like "The Dragon," Bruce Lee undeniably lived at the top of the martial arts pyramid. So, when a powerhouse like him laid down at the age of 32 and never woke again, the world was stunned. One of the most in-depth biographies on Lee makes the assertion that he "wasn't just an entertainer; he was an evangelist." That's quite a testament to Bruce Lee's impact on other people and their decisions to embark upon a lifelong journey with martial arts.

It seemed as though Bruce Lee could take down a fiery dragon if faced with one. Yet, he died on July 20, 1973 -- at the tender age of 32.

How could a man of enviable strength and skill just drop dead in his early thirties? Really, how did Bruce Lee die?

The Death of a Dragon

Lee's final [film, *Enter the Dragon*,] went down in history as one of the most successful martial arts movies of all time. In fact, his hand strikes were so [fast] the camera speed had to be adjusted. During its filming, on May 10, 1973, Lee collapsed and was rushed to Hong Kong Baptist Hospital. The doctors diagnosed him with cerebral [edema] or brain swelling due to excess fluid. They reduced the swelling by administering mannitol, a drug known to decrease intracranial pressure, but this wasn't the last Lee would succumb to the treachery of cerebral edema.

On July 20, 1973, Lee met with producer Raymond Chow and then drove to actress Betty Ting Pei's house to go over their scripts. After Lee complained of a headache, Ting gave him some Equagesic, a pill containing aspirin and a tranquilizer. Lee took the tablet, laid down for a nap, and never woke again.

Bruce Lee's death was ruled "death by misadventure." Coroners stated he had a severe allergic reaction to the tranquilizer in Equagesic, causing his brain to swell. When you consider his May hospitalization, it all seemed to add up.[89]

While many other theories have been presented as to the cause of Lee's death, many believe that brain swelling due to excess fluid caused by one of the ingredients in the pill was the ultimate cause.

Life is uncertain, but God isn't. In the book of Ephesians, we're told that God has given us two things at salvation that can never be taken away from us. Please turn there in your Bible and we'll find out what these are.

Ephesians 1:7

> *In whom we have redemption through his blood, the*
> *forgiveness of sins, according to the riches of his grace;*

In whom (Christ), you *have redemption* (to let one go free; separation from all of the consequences of our transgressions) *through his blood* (the price paid to satisfy divine justice) and *the forgiveness* (to blot out; not to remember any longer; to throw a person's sins behind one's back; to carry away your sins so that they might never again be seen) *of sins.*

On the cross, Christ paid the penalty and provided forgiveness for the sins of the whole world (1 John 2:2). However, at salvation, the verb *have* gives us further clarification about *redemption* and *forgiveness.* These words in Koine Greek are in the form of a present active indicative.

What this conveys to us is that you, who are saved, are in full and continuous possession of[90] redemption and forgiveness.

There will be some that will say because you've committed such and such sins that the payment for sin and its forgiveness can be undone. It can't. *Your redemption of deliverance from the wrath of God and the release from sin's hold*[91] *and forgiveness (no written accusation stands against [you] because [your] sins have been taken away*[92]*) is your continuous possession.* Praise God!

This doesn't mean that grace gives us a license to sin. It means that God has provided us with the grace that will teach us how to deny ungodliness and worldly lusts (Titus 2:12). And hopefully, we'll choose to learn what grace has to say about such and apply it to our new lives.

Have you ever wished that you could go back and start your life over again? Well, if you're a believer, you actually have. If you're not a believer, then what you'll find out in the following chapter is how this can become a reality in your life.

13

YOU ARE A NEW CREATURE

Have you ever caught up with someone you hadn't seen for many years who committed a serious criminal offense and were shocked to see how their life had changed for the better? Here's an article that exemplifies this.

FREE TO SUCCEED: NAOMI BLOUNT

"Over the years, [I've] written my obituary numerous times," says Naomi Blount. "I never thought [I'd] ever be coming home." That's because in 1982, she was sentenced to life in Pennsylvania state prison. She was [thirty-two] years old.

A drug addict and alcoholic, Naomi struggled every day of her adult life. One terrible day, a man stabbed her friend, Brenda Baker. The two women then found the man and wanted to hurt him, but it was Brenda who delivered the fatal injury, not Naomi. In Pennsylvania, you don't have to be the one who committed homicide to get charged with the crime; you just have to have been there in a certain capacity.

Behind bars with no release in sight, Naomi's tough situation was matched by grit and determination to improve herself. Her son, [ten] years old when she went inside, meant everything to Naomi, and for his sake, she vowed that even though she was supposed to die in prison, she would be leaving the world a better person than when she'd entered it. She earned several degrees, stayed clean, and helped others.

"I wanted my son to, at least when he picked up my body, I wanted him to know that his mother was more than an alcoholic and a drug addict."

Naomi applied for and was denied commutation five times. About to give up, she hand-wrote a heartfelt plea to the Board of Pardons, begging them to reconsider. Then, in the equivalent of winning a lottery ticket, she was granted clemency – almost unheard of in Pennsylvania. She'd been in prison [thirty-seven] years.

Remarkably, now [seventy-two], Naomi is not bitter. In the three years since she's been released, it seems as though there's [nothing,] she hasn't been able to accomplish. [She's] a vocal advocate for reform, and she also works as a commutation specialist for the Commonwealth of Pennsylvania. "My job allows me to encourage those that are on the inside," she says.

She's very close to her son, now [fifty], and his family. "I'm getting ready to be a great-grandmother for the second time," Naomi says. "This will be the first baby that [I'm] home for." And the passion for music that she has had her whole life has flourished. Recently, she released an album, called "Mello-D" by Simply Naomi.

She also works as a program consultant for a group that helped her when she was inside, Shining Light. They provide support to people in prison.

Naomi is herself a "shining light," trying every day to express what she feels deeply: gratitude. "I'm always saying, 'Lord, thank you. Thank you, God. Thank you, [God.]'"[93]

As Naomi was given clemency, a pardon after many years in prison, so have you been granted such by someone who knows everything about you. Even though the penalty for sin has been taken care of and the record of such forgiven by Jesus Christ's atonement on the cross, this hasn't changed the fallen nature that deprives everyone from having an intimate relationship with God.

Fortunately, God knows how to take each person out from their perpetual bondage by giving them an opportunity to respond to the message of a new life, i.e., of a new nature that can be theirs. And if and when they make this decision, a pronouncement will be made relating to them which is found in the book of 2 Corinthians. Let's go there and find out what this announcement is all about.

2 Corinthians 5:17

> *Therefore if any man be in Christ, he is a new creature: old things are passed away; behold, all things are become new.*

You're described as being *in Christ*, which [speaks of your spiritual relationship to Him because you] believed the message of the gospel and was identified by faith with Him.[94] Thus, if this is the case, and it is, then you're *a new creature, a new creation, a new person on the inside.*[95] Did you hear that? You're a new being, a child of God!

As such, *old things* (selfish, carnal views of ourselves, of others, and of Christ;[96] those things that characterized the pre-Christian life[97]) have *passed away* (disappeared) and your whole sphere of being has become new, whom God the Father owns as [His] workmanship, and which he can look on and pronounce very good.[98]

God doesn't see you as you see yourself at times as falling short, as never going to change, as being hopeless in this or that aspect of your life. This doesn't mean that He's unaware of your sinful tendencies. However, this doesn't take away from His recognition of you as His son or daughter as was His perception of David when God sent Samuel to the house of Jesse to anoint him the next king of Israel.

> *1 Samuel 16:7 But the Lord said unto Samuel, Look not on his countenance, or on the height of his stature; because I have refused him: for the Lord seeth not as man seeth; for man*

> *looketh on the outward appearance, but the Lord looketh on the heart.*

So, find out what God's declaration is of you in His Word regarding every area of your new life and begin to think of yourself as to the new person you've become. Remind yourself that you've been given a new nature even though the reality of such in your thinking, speaking, and acting hasn't been worked out yet. *And remember, [you're] a new creation, a new man, a work of the divine power as decided and as glorious as when God created all things out of nothing,*[99] *with new views, new motives, new principles, new [objectives] and plans of life.*[100]

Before we take a look at another beautiful description of our new lives in Christ in the next section, I'd like to leave you with this quote from Barnes Notes that accentuates what we've just talked about.

The idea evidently is, not that he ought to be a new creature, but that he is in fact; not that he ought to live as becomes a new creature - which is true enough - but that [he'll] in fact live in that way, and manifest the characteristics of the new creation.[101]

Prior to your conversion to Christ, was there ever anything that you longed for that you believed would provide you with happiness but always seemed to be outside of your grasp? There was one lifelong endeavor of mine that I only found in Christ. What was it?

14

YOU ARE ACCEPTED

I don't know about you, but when I was growing up, it seemed like I never fit in. My dad, for whatever reason, moved my family to different locations quite a bit. In most cases, I believe it was related to his job. So, I never had the chance to make friends and be in their life over an extended period of time. And being an only child, I didn't have a brother or sister to confide in.

In my teen years, I longed for acceptance by my peers, whoever they might be. At this time in my life, my father opened a spa and grille business in what was considered to be the epicenter of crime in my hometown. I'd work for him after school and soon became friends with many of those in the neighborhood.

Most of them would meet up in a nearby park, usually in the evening hours, and would gather together for food, alcohol, drugs, and sex. At first, this was quite an alarming lifestyle, as I was attending a private Catholic high school whose values taught were contrary to what was taking place in this environment. Eventually, I began to partake in what everyone else was doing in the group.

My dad disapproved of my choice of friends and this caused friction at work and home. I longed to leave the household and live on my own to have the freedom to do what I wanted. While I did attend college after high school, I'd still party with my contemporaries on the weekends.

And then it all came crashing down. After receiving a college degree to teach high school mathematics, I was unsuccessful in getting a job. I broke up with a young lady I'd been dating over something foolish. Many of my associates had gotten married, which limited my interaction with them. And my relationship with my father remained strained.

I needed assistance. I felt isolated. I longed for a new start. I remember the times in my younger years when my parents would take me to church. I wondered if the God I heard about in the messages from the pulpit could change my life. So, I decided once a week, beginning with the church I attended as a little kid, to visit the many other faiths in my home city to find out if the God they believed in could help me personally.

And then it happened. On the Sunday of a holiday weekend, I'd just gotten out of working for my dad at his business. A parade in honor of the celebration was passing by. So, I decided to walk behind it until it dispersed at the city's town hall. As I was about to turn around and walk back to my father's store, where my car was parked, I heard a loud noise in the distance.

What appeared was a gathering of people standing before a platform where someone was talking on a microphone over a loudspeaker. As I got closer, a young man was talking about God. He said there's one true God who wants to be your best friend. He wants to come into your life and give you a new nature. He wants to guide you. He wants to be involved in every aspect of your life. And then he proclaimed the gospel of repentance and faith for whosoever will.

While there's more to this story, eventually, I responded to what was said, and immediately I was saturated with a wave of divine love, peace, and joy. What I realize now is that at this time and forever more, I became accepted by Him, just like you were accepted at salvation. Approved in what sense? Please go to the book of Ephesians, and we'll find out.

. . .

Ephesians 1:6

To the praise of the glory of his grace, wherein he hath made us accepted in the beloved.

You should *praise* God the Father because *of the glory* (the glorious manifestation[102]) *of his grace* (the revelation of his unmerited love[103]) *wherein he* had *made* you *accepted* (freely bestowed on [you the grace which saved you],[104] when you responded to it; by which He honored you with blessings). These favors could refer to the many irrevocable absolutes received at salvation that we've been looking at in this study.

What we know about the word *accepted* is that it's a verb in Koine Greek in the form of an aorist active indicative. The aorist tense in this context is considered as constative meaning that this acceptance views something in its entirety. With that said, this verse could be described by saying that God the Father acknowledges you in the beloved whereby you were bestowed in its completeness all spiritual blessings at the point in time in the past when you responded to the gospel.

And finally, this acceptance is *in the beloved* (in the sphere of the Lord Jesus, His [Person, and work] on the Cross[105]).

So, remember, at salvation, God the Father has accepted you, i.e., made you the subject of His grace and freely bestowed upon you irrevocable spiritual benefits. Thank you, God!

Are you ready to find out what another one of these special honors is that has been bestowed upon you? I am. Onward Christian soldier.

15

YOU ARE WASHED

Have you ever been deceived (mislead by false appearance or statement[106])? Countless commercials are broadcast on TV or social media telling us that such and such product is the best ever. That you can't live without it.

And then we're continually bombarded with broadcasts that ask for money for whatever cause. Whether the money will be used for what they say it's intended, we'll never know. How many of us have believed a lie without knowing that we have? I'll admit to it.

Well, here's an amazing story about deception that you won't believe could actually happen, but it did.

ONLINE LOVE TRIANGLE, DECEPTION [ENDS] IN MURDER
Chatroom flirtation leads to [a] deadly relationship.
[Aug. 27, 2011 & #151]; -- The Internet is known as a breeding ground for illicit affairs between [people,] often hiding behind fake names and handles. But most such virtual relationships aren't dangerous as this -- when "Talhotblond" and "MarineSniper" struck up a relationship online, it ended in murder.

MarineSniper was [46 years old,] Thomas Montgomery, a married father of two. In [May] 2005, posing as a young, handsome Iraq-bound Marine, he entered a teen chat room [of] the popular game site "Pogo." When 18-year-old Talhotblond started [instant messaging him, he decided to pretend he was 18, too.] "I kept thinking, well, we're never going to meet. ... I'll just play the game with her," he said. Before long, the flirtation became a romance.

Talhotblond's instant messages revealed that her real name was Jessi, a softball-playing high school senior from West Virginia. She sent Montgomery photos that lived up to her screen name ... and then some. "There were some ... very provocative poses," he said. In return, Jessi wanted to see what he looked like [too,] so he sent her his photo from Marine boot camp. The picture was 30 years out of date. Montgomery's screen name, Marinesniper, was a nostalgic harkening back to the six years he spent in the military as a young man. He has hinted darkly of covert ops and dark deeds best unmentioned, but U.S. Marine records obtained by "20/20" show that although he qualified as a sharpshooter, he never trained as a sniper or saw action.

But for Jessi, he invented a younger, stronger, more virile version of [himself] called [*Tommy*.] "He was my height, 6 feet tall, had bright red hair," said Montgomery, "big shoulders, muscles and all that." Instant messages recovered from his computer show that the online relationship began to consume Montgomery. He told "20/20" that this relationship "became more real to me than real life." The feeling seemed to be mutual. Jessi and "Tommy" exchanged gifts, phone [calls,] and love letters. "I love you always and forever, Tommy," wrote Jessi. "[I've] never felt this way," Montgomery responded.

["The relationship had become more than flirtatious,"] Montgomery said. "There was virtual sex going on in there between her and Tommy," he said. While Montgomery said the virtual sex made him "feel kind of dirty," he was in too deep to sever ties with her. "If I was smart, I would've just ended it, but it was like a, a drug that I needed every day," he said. Montgomery seemed to be losing touch with reality. He wrote a note to himself: "On January 2, 2006 Tom Montgomery (46 years old) ceases to exist and is replaced by [an

18-year-old battle-scarred marine ... He's] moving to West Virginia to be with the love of his life."

Online Fantasy World Crashes

Fate finally took a hand. In March 2006, Montgomery told "20/20" one of his daughters was using his computer when Jessi happened to instant message him. Montgomery's wife, alerted by her daughter, found a trove of love letters, [photos,] and mementos from Jessi, including a pair of red panties. She sent Jessi a photo of her family and a letter.

"Let me introduce you to these people," she wrote. "The man in the center is Tom, my husband since 1989. ... He is 46 years old." Montgomery said Jessi was [horrified] and broke off the relationship immediately. "She sends me a text message and [says] she hates me ... you should be put in jail for this," he told "20/20." But Jessi also e-mailed one of Montgomery's co-workers, a 22-year-old, [good-looking], part-time machinist and college student named Brian Barrett, to see if it was really true.

Brian's screen name is ["Beefcake,"] and as he consoled Jessi online, she seemed to find a better fit with him -- and perhaps a way to strike back at the combat Marine who wasn't. Before long, Jessi was sending Brian her [photos, and the two had become a cyber item]. Marinesniper became consumed with jealousy -- and he wasn't about to take it lying down.

"Brian will pay in blood," Montgomery instant messaged Jessi at one point. His messages became increasingly [violent] as he was forced to watch their romance blossom in the same chat rooms he used to frequent with Jessi. "He was enraged," said former prosecutor Ken Case. "I mean, it oftentimes shocked me when I saw the names that he would call her."

Jessi and Berrett took to the Internet to make sure everyone knew Montgomery (who recently had a birthday) was a liar. "They were then going into these chat [rooms] and letting people know that he was actually 47 years old," said Case. "They almost made him out to be a pedophile." But the IMs that came from Talhotblond showed her to be torn --- mad one instant, desperate to return to a love with a man who she knew didn't exist ... teasing him.

She [continued talking] to Montgomery online:

Talhotblond: i ache to be with tommy
    Talhotblond: do you miss it tom
    Marinesniper: more then u will ever know
    Marinesniper: my heart aches to hear you call me your tommie
    Marinesniper: i wish i could be that 19 yr old marine for u
    Talhotblond: i know tom

Talhotblond Rekindles Cyberaffair

Jessi took up with Montgomery again. "In his mind, this was the jackpot," said Barbara Schroeder, who documented the bizarre relationship in a documentary called [*Talhotblond*.] "He was being accepted for being 47, and he still had this hot young girl who wanted him." Montgomery knew he was in way over his head, but he couldn't bring himself to end things with her.

"It was like a drug. I was addicted to it," he said. "I [couldn't just] end it." At one point, when his wife actually told him to get off the computer and talk to her, Montgomery couldn't. "I just told her I'll get off when I'm done," he recalled. Montgomery says nothing sexual happened between them after Talhotblond found out how old he was, but their IMs tell a different story:

Marinesniper: wish you were nude
    Talhotblond: what would ya do?

Marinesniper: stare
    Talhotblond: that all

Marinesniper: nope
Marinesniper: u might get the magic

Talhotblond: mmmmm
Talhotblond: make love to me tommy

But it didn't last. Jessi told Montgomery they were [through] and seemed to take up with Barrett again. Montgomery began to go into a downward spiral. "The obsession turns into jealousy, and then the jealousy turns into betrayal and revenge," said District Attorney Frank Sedita. "You really start to [get a] sense of this person going into an abyss. And it's kind of frightening."

And then... the tipping point. Barrett said he was going to meet Talhotblond -- in person. "He actually drove down to, I [think, North Carolina," said prosecutor] Case. "And on his way back, he was saying, 'I'm going right past your house. I'd love to get [together.'"] Jessi texted him at the last minute not to visit, but Montgomery, who had learned of the plan to meet, was incensed.

On Sept. 15, 2006, as Barrett left work, three shots rang out. Brian Barrett was found dead in the parking lot where he worked, shot three times by a military rifle. Police quickly learned of the Internet love triangle from co-workers. And when they couldn't find Thomas Montgomery, they feared they knew just where he was headed. "At three in the morning," Capt. Ron Kenyon told ["20/20," our] first concern was talking to Jessi and making sure she was still alive. But when police arrived at her home, they were in for another surprise: A woman named Mary Shieler opened the door.

Talhotblond's Shocking Secret
As police questioned her, she revealed a shocking truth: She was

the one who had been sending messages to Montgomery and Barrett under the handle Talhotblond. The pictures she sent Montgomery were actually those of her daughter, the real Jessi, who had no knowledge of her mother's cyberlife.

Montgomery was charged and later [pleaded] guilty to the murder of Brian Barrett. In exchange for his plea, he received a 20-year sentence. Prosecutors said their discovery of Montgomery's DNA on a peach pit found at the crime scene and a photo of [the] Montgomery family's gun cabinet -- which showed the type of old military rifle that police believe was used to shoot Barrett -- were key to their case against Montgomery.

Prosecutors in Buffalo, meanwhile, looked for a way to charge Mary Shieler for something -- anything -- in the case but concluded she may have [trampled] all over the moral and ethical [line] but never crossed the legal one. "Shame on her -- she not only didn't do anything about it, I think she provoked it," said Ken Case. "[Unfortunately,] in New York State, you have to do a little something more to be criminally liable."

Mary Shieler didn't come away unscathed. Her husband divorced her over her [deception,] and her daughter Jessi cut [ties,] too, moving in with relatives in Virginia, where she was attending college. Mary Shieler also pursued an education -- she took classes at a community college in West Virginia. She has spoken publicly about the deadly love triangle just once, to the BBC. "It was stupid. It should have never happened. I just never thought it would go anywhere," she said. "That it would end, fall [off,] and that would be the end of it."[107]

After reading this article, it's difficult to believe that so many people weren't only deceived but willing to throw away everything to fulfill a fantasy. In the Christian life, we too, have to be extremely careful. There will be false teachers who'll try to convince us that certain behaviors are approved by God. Let's see what the Apostle Paul has to say about this. Please turn in your Bibles to the book of 1 Corinthians.

. . .

1 Corinthians 6:9-11

> *Know ye not that the unrighteous shall not inherit the kingdom of God? Be not deceived: neither fornicators, nor idolaters, nor adulterers, nor effeminate, nor abusers of themselves with mankind, Nor thieves, nor covetous, nor drunkards, nor revilers, nor extortioners, shall inherit the kingdom of God. And such were some of you: but ye are washed, but ye are sanctified, but ye are justified in the name of the Lord Jesus, and by the Spirit of our God.*

There were a couple of things that the Apostle Paul addressed in 1 Corinthians chapter 6. One of them was whether a believer should take another believer to court before unbelievers (1 Corinthians 6:1-8). The second had to do with salvation and egregious sins. He began by making a straightforward statement. The *unrighteous* (those who aren't children of God) *shall not inherit* (take possession of; not enter into) *the kingdom of God* (the spiritual kingdom).

And then, he followed this up with a statement that appears to cause much confusion in church circles. What he seemed to be saying was, if someone habitually commits any one of these sins, they'll not enter into the kingdom of God. The sins, he discloses, that would inhibit their entrance are as follows.

- Fornicators - those who have sex outside of marriage
- Idolators - anyone who worships an image of a deity
- Adulterers - sex with someone who's not your husband or wife
- Effeminate - those who make self-indulgence the grand object of life
- Abusers of themselves with mankind – "the passive and active partners... in male homosexual relation" (Barrett)[108]
- Thieves - those who [take advantage] of their brethren by any kind of fraud or secret artifice [trick][109]
- Covetous - eager for gain; greedy

- Drunkards – those who are habitually drunk
- Revilers - gossipers and slanderers
- Extortioners - those that violently seize on another's wealth[110]

Some commentators and fellow believers with whom I've had discussions about such matters have suggested that if a Christian is continually sinning in any of these areas, then they'll lose their salvation, or it's surmised they were never saved in the first place. I think that the key to interpreting this verse is by looking at the words at the beginning, which are, *be not deceived*. The verb *deceived* can also mean to be misled, i.e., to lead into [the] error of conduct, thought, or judgment.[111]

It's true then, as it is now. How many people don't consider some of these actions as sins? The *unrighteous* (the unsaved) hopefully had the gospel presented to them but chose not to repent (to change their views, designs, and practices[112]). That disqualified them from being allowed to enter the kingdom of God. But some take this a step further to mean that if you, a believer, likewise choose to practice these sins regularly, then you'll also not be allowed to enter in. Do you agree with this perception? The key again in interpreting these passages is *be not deceived.*

The apostle concludes by saying, *And such were some of you,* i.e., some of you had continually or repeatedly committed some of these sinful actions before you were saved. But at a point in time, at salvation, you repented and believed in Christ, and subsequently, it's a statement of fact that *you are washed*, or rather you had yourself washed by the Holy Spirit. The word *washed* means to be made pure. By the agency of the [Spirit,] the defilement of these pollutions had been washed away or removed.[113] Another meaning for *washed* is that it's the setting apart of one as consecrated [dedicated to the service or worship of a deity[114]] by the Spirit in the eternal purpose of God.[115]

With that said, keep in mind the phrase *be not deceived.* What seems to be going on here is the Apostle Paul was contrasting salvation to unbelievers and sanctification with believers. On the one hand, he emphasized certain sins because they were considered acceptable according to societal standards. However, when someone gets saved, they become *washed*. Does this infer that they couldn't go back and commit any of these sins again? No, it doesn't. But this doesn't change the fact that they're *washed*.

Do you know that there's no such thing as a lying or fornicating or gay Christian, etc., but there's such a thing as a Christian who lies, commits fornication, engages in homosexual acts, etc.? Huh? Who you are, including your new identity in Christ, isn't impacted by carrying out certain transgressions. However, there's no question that your walk with God will be affected.

So, don't continue to regard or think of your spiritual integrity according to your engagement in a certain sin or sins because God doesn't. Confess them and apply God's prescription concerning it, i.e., His Word. *And remind yourself daily, I'm washed, I'm pure and I'm set apart as someone committed by the Holy Spirit to devotion in the plan of God.* Amen.

One of the most misunderstood blessings you've inherited is what we'll look at next. Any idea what this might pertain to regarding your new life in Christ?

16

YOU ARE DEAD TO SIN

*D*id you know that there was a time when someone who was pronounced dead really wasn't? And because of such, after the person was buried, certain accommodations were made so that if they returned to life, they could make contact with others from outside the grave. Here's an article for you to read that pertains to such. And by the way, the state where this story originated from is Ohio.

GRAVE BELLS INDICATED 'THE DECEASED' WERE ALIVE

NEW MATAMORAS - Most people wouldn't give [a] second thought to a bell ringing. But in the 19th century, a ringing bell could mean the dead weren't. Someone unintentionally buried alive would pull the string in the coffin to ring a bell at topside.

"The bell's purpose was if they (unintentionally) buried you alive, you were supposed to feel around the coffin...for a string," John Miller, president of the Matamoras Historical Society, said. "You were supposed to ring that [bell. Grave bells were believed to have been used at the Cooper Cemetery near the Monroe County line on Rinard

Mills Road. It could be the origins behind the saying of *saved by the bell*,"] he said.

Miller said usually a pipe led down through the ground and into the coffin. A string ran from the coffin and outside to the bell. People watched the cemetery just in case a bell was rung, then the person who had been buried alive would be rescued.

He said without more modern technology some people with very low pulse rates and breathing rates [could be] buried alive. There was also no embalming. "Often people were pronounced dead and they weren't really," Miller said. "You would wake up and [you're] in your grave. It makes the hair on your neck stand up."

The story of the Cooper Cemetery bell has circulated for years between nearby residents. The evidence of a bell was reported to be a pipe sticking up from the ground next to one of the headstones in the [back-left] corner of the cemetery. While the evidence of this pipe is no longer visible, its story lingers.

According to Miller, Cooper Cemetery was established in 1821 with its first burial of Nancy Pugh. "There were no burials until [thirty] years later in 1851," he said. "All three of them were late in the fall and this is where they got the name Cooper Cemetery." The next three burials were of Elisha Cooper, 60 at his death, Mary Cooper, 8, and John Cooper, 2. The most recent burial was of Perley McKnight in November 2012.

Though Cooper Cemetery's bell has long since disappeared without a trace, its legacy continues to live on. Jim Moore, 61, of Little Hocking used to live near Cooper Cemetery in his youth. Though he hasn't been around the cemetery for years, he still remembers hearing about and looking for the bell. "I remember when I was a kid talking with dad," Moore said. "He told me about it. The grave was kind of sunken in the [back-left] corner of the cemetery. There was definitely something there my dad pointed out. It was like a hole with a pipe type of deal."

Moore said the story of the cemetery's bell has had a lasting effect. "You know how when you're a kid, it's all kind of spooky," Moore said. "It was always something I remembered. It's kind of surprising and it's just one of those things that's just stuck in my mind."[116]

Can you imagine someone who has been buried alive, was able to ring the bell, and heard a faint voice from outside letting them know that they'll get them out. And after a while hearing what appears to be digging taking place above with the anticipation of being rescued. As the coffin was brought up and opened, I'm sure they crawled out with surprise and thankfulness wondering how they got there in the first place.

Their next response might be, I can't wait to get home. Can someone please take me home? And when they got to the front door and knocked what surprise and shock awaited whosoever opened it.

Well, I think a similar response takes place from fellow believers when they hear the news about the next blessing that has been received by each of them at salvation. It's one of those benefits that many won't accept. Please turn to the book of Romans and we'll find out what this is about.

Romans 6:1-2

> *1 What shall we say then? Shall we continue in sin, that grace may abound?*

The Apostle Paul was instructing the Christians in Rome concerning sin and grace. He asked them, should we *continue* to *sin* habitually, so that *grace* (the divine influence upon the heart, and its reflection in the life[117]) *may abound* (shall increase)? In other words, should believers sin all the more so that the elements of character of the Spirit will increasingly develop?

> *2 God forbid. How shall we, that are dead to sin, live any longer therein?*

His response was *God forbid*, i.e., no, just the opposite. Grace doesn't expand the more a believer sins. Sin inhibits the ministry of the Holy Spirit. What this revealed was either a lack of clear teaching about grace or the grace taught wasn't being appropriated. So, what does grace teach us in regard to sin? This is found in the book of Titus.

> *Titus 2:12 Teaching us that, denying ungodliness and worldly lusts, we should live soberly, righteously, and godly, in this present world;*

Grace teaches us to deny ungodliness and worldly lusts.

Another thing that Paul reminded them of was that at salvation, another spiritual reality had taken place in their life, which is that they were *dead to sin*. This can be restated in a few different ways. It can mean to be separated from sin's power, not the extinction of sin;[118] that sin has lost its influence; death to the old life in sin;[119] or to be separated once and for all from the sinful nature.[120]

And if this is the case, and it is, then Paul goes on to say, how shall we *live any longer therein? What he means is, as to our position in Christ, we can't continue to live in sin because we're dead to it.* So, accept this new reality about yourself.

This isn't saying that a believer can't sin, but in our standing in Christ, we're dead to it. Why is this truth so important to understand? It's because as we've already discussed earlier in this study, there are teachings which claim that if a believer commits habitual sin, then they'll lose their salvation, or their sinful life will indicate that they were never born again in the first place. This is of such paramount importance to the new person you've become and whether sin could impact it that we took an in depth look at this earlier in chapter 4. So, if you need refreshing as to whether sin could impact salvation in either perspective, then I'd recommend going back there and rereading this section over again.

As far as whether it's possible for a believer to continually commit sin after they're saved, the verb *continue* from the prior verse will provide for us an answer to such. The word *continue* in Koine Greek is in the form of a present active subjunctive. This tells us that a believer can choose to continually live in sin. However, in their position they're dead to it. Their seating in Christ remains, although in their experience their conduct acts in contradiction to their new state. Their salvation is still there but there's no witness of such.

So, what you've learned is that nothing can change this new reality in your life, i.e., you're dead to sin because you're in Christ. And because of such, sin has lost its influence [over you; you're] not subject to it; [you're] in regard to that, as the [person] in the grave is to the busy scenes and cares of this life.[121] And as you've been made aware how to address sin, which is by means of a process called sanctification, this positional reality will be worked out in your life and become increasingly evident to you.

Another favor that we'll look at has to do with a blessing that I'd say most people in this world desire. Any guesses what this could be?

17

YOU ARE BELOVED

I think you'd agree with me when I say that most people want to be loved. When we look for the right one, somehow, we have specific criteria that we look for: good looks, tall or short, rich, athletic, similar hobbies, fat or skinny, adventurous, free spirit, like-minded, funny, member of the same faith or political affiliation, etc. And if somehow the relationship becomes fulfilling, the couple decides to either live together or get married.

Along the way, situations will come up. Some are financial; others might involve physical, verbal, and/or emotional abuse, not being faithful, alcohol or drug issues, not being honest, declining physical health, not wanting to have children, sexual indifference, lack of communication, etc. Unfortunately, for many, separation or divorce is the result. We live in a world where love is desired, and yet when it wanes, it's most often why so many people no longer remain together for one reason or another.

Here are some interesting statistics on divorce.

The current divorce rate in the US is 2.3 persons per 1,000 people. Overall, the rate of divorces in America is falling. Divorces amongst people aged 50+ years are rising. Fewer couples choose to marry than pre-1990. The most common causes of divorce are conflict, arguing, irretrievable breakdown in the relationship, lack of commitment, infidelity, and lack of physical intimacy.[122]

So, what is it that might help to keep the marriage union together? I found an interesting article on this topic. Let's take a few minutes and see what it has to say.

HOW TO GET LOST IN GOD'S LOVE AND SAVE YOUR MARRIAGE

Every person on earth has a deep desire to be loved. And as wonderful as love in marriage is, it will never be a fulfilling love unless we first saturate ourselves in the unfailing love of God.

"Lord, fix my husband. Fix us!" As quickly as the prayer was on my lips, I felt God ask, *Do you believe I can do what [you're] asking Me to do?*

I did not.

My husband, Bob, and I had reached a place of deep pain. Busyness. Sinfulness. Selfishness. I was angry with Bob. The circumstances don't really matter. They're probably a lot like the circumstances in your marriage from time to time. But convinced I [couldn't] love him well until he loved me better, I dug myself into a prayer routine that proved futile.

I was, in fact, looking for love in the wrong place. *As wonderful as love in marriage is, it will never be a fulfilling love unless we first saturate ourselves in the unfailing love of God.*

Before you accuse me of sounding cliché, I've learned this on the hot pavement of life, and I'd like to offer four practical tips that have helped me to live it out.

ADMIT THAT WHAT YOU NEED MORE THAN ANYTHING ELSE IN THIS WORLD IS TO BE WELL LOVED.

Because love is a basic need of humanity, every person has a deep desire to be loved. During a difficult season of feeling unloved in my marriage, God led me to Proverbs 19:22 (NIV): "What a person desires is unfailing love; better to be poor than a liar."

The Bible uses the phrase "unfailing love" more than [thirty] times, and not one of them refers to any source other than God himself. He alone holds the answer to our deep craving for love. *This means that your husband or wife will never be able to fulfill this need unless you first find satisfaction in God's love.*

LET YOUR SPOUSE OFF THE HOOK.

The greatest symptom that my need for love was misdirected was that I was praying for God to change my husband — without having the humility to ask God how He wanted to change me. [It's] never wrong to pray for God to make your husband or wife more like Him. However, when your prayers are void of your own need, that might indicate you're trying to have your needs met through a person's love rather than through God's. When I realized this in my own life, I simply asked God to make me hungry for *His* love.

It takes a lot of courage to admit that your marriage might not be exactly what you want because [you're] not exactly what you need to be. Be brave. Put yourself under God's care to be changed.

WRITE A LIST OF THINGS YOUR SPOUSE DOES TO EXPRESS HIS OR HER LOVE FOR YOU.

Do this as an act of thanksgiving to God. My counselor assigned this task to me and, although I took it on reluctantly, it had a dramatic impact on my heart. I am, in fact, a very loved woman. I have a husband who never fails to ask for forgiveness, prays with me each night at bedtime, willingly enters into counseling when we need it, manages our money well, begs me to sneak away with him from time to time, and tolerates my weaknesses as much as I tolerate his. It's easy to lose sight of all this when we're hurting each other, and [it's] so important to refocus our thinking to be grateful. As I did this, it became an act of loving my husband through God's love in me.

. . .

INVEST IN THE FRIENDSHIP OF YOUR SPOUSE.

This world's paradigm of love can often put a lot of emphasis on sex, [romance,] and passion in marriage. If those things aren't on full boil, we tend to think our relationship lacks love. *But God's Word defines marital love more in terms of friendship and commitment than sex and romance.* Take a night to play a board game or enjoy a hike together on a Sunday afternoon. If you can meet your spouse for lunch, consider canceling an appointment with a personal trainer or even a friend.

I've long embraced the biblical story of the woman at the well (John 4). She tried man after man but never felt that her thirst for love had been quenched. She was desperate and love-sick. Then, when Jesus showed up, He offered her the love she really needed. But she said, "You have nothing to draw water with, and the well is [deep."]

How like us! How like me. You don't have to be a woman who has had many husbands to be parched with a thirst for love. You just have to be a woman [who's] trying to get something from her husband that only God can give. I know. [I've] been there many times, just waiting for God to show up. And when He does, I'm prone to tell him, "But God, I'm in *so deep,* and you don't have a bucket!"

It doesn't matter how deep the problem; the solution is still God's love. And He has buckets and buckets of love to fix your marriage. And to fix your heart.[123]

Since the fall of Adam and Eve, relationships have been fractured. Each of us has a sin nature that contains passions or tendencies that evidence, in some instances, more good human traits than bad or worse human traits than good. The causes are varied, such as the fallen nature, genetics, family upbringing, peer group affiliations, etc.

Along with this, there have been countless books on how to save a relationship. It's unfortunate that when a marriage deteriorates, we tend to look at our partner differently. No longer as the one who's our teammate, our best friend, our confidant but as an enemy. How much child support are they requesting? How much of what we own together will they want? Who will have custody of the children? And what will the visitation rights be?

But when we become a child of God, a verse from the book of Colossians tells us how He continually chooses to treat us no matter how we've chosen to treat Him.

Colossians 3:12

> *Put on therefore, as the elect of God, holy and beloved, bowels of mercies, kindness, humbleness of mind, meekness, longsuffering;*

Did you know that at salvation, God calls you, the *elect, beloved*? Let's begin by clarifying what it means for you to be called God's *elect*. God has chosen you, *the elect*, to salvation as those who would believe [in] his Son.[124] Why did God single you out in eternity past? He didn't choose you because He chose some to heaven and others to hell. You were chosen because He knew beforehand that when the gospel was presented to you in your time on earth, you'd decide to respond to it.

Another misperception as to why God selects certain ones is as some might say is because of their excellent works. Clarification concerning this misconception is found in the following verse from the book of Ephesians.

> *Ephesians 2:8-9 For by grace are ye saved through faith; and that not of yourselves: it is the gift of God: Not of works, lest any man should boast.*

And because of your unmerited response, i.e., not of works to the gospel of grace, God declares you *holy* (you're standing in grace as someone set apart from the world unto the Lord),[125] and *beloved* (dearly loved; this is God's love, … a love that denies self for the benefit of the object loved).[126]

The word *beloved* is a verb that, in Koine Greek, is in the form of a perfect passive participle.

With this designation, we could rewrite this verse and state it this way. When you responded to God the Father's invitation of salvation, you, the elect, at this point in time, became profoundly loved and the reality *of God loving you personally continues with the present result that [you are the object] of His love.*[127]

And as you learn about the spiritual qualities of God's love and apply them to yourself, you'll begin to express these self-less qualities for the benefit of your believing or unbelieving husband or wife, friends, enemies, associates at work, fellow believers, unbelievers, those that have hurt you, etc. Whether they receive this love doesn't change the love of God that's emanating from your life. And no matter what the ultimate result is of these relationships, you'll evidence to them what the Bible says is of great gain.

1 Timothy 6:6 But godliness with contentment is great gain.

Godliness with contentment is an inner sufficiency that keeps us at peace in spite of outward circumstances.[128]

Have you ever bought something and said something like, it's perfect? In my younger years, there was something that I had the same sentiment about. What was it and what's the spiritual blessing associated with it? Please continue on, and we'll soon find out.

18

YOU ARE COMPLETE

When you think of the word *complete*, what comes to your mind? For me, this word means that whatever it is, it has all that I'm looking for. When I turned sixteen, I attended driving school. After successfully completing it, my father told me that he'd like to buy me a starter car. So, once a week we'd go to different car dealerships looking at used cars.

It seemed like everywhere we went, I couldn't make up my mind. They were all nice, but none of them piqued my interest until as we were driving into another dealership, there it was. It caught my attention. I was in car love. It was complete. The year was 1967. Any idea what car I was looking at? Think of a horse. You guessed it.

It was a 1967 Ford Mustang GT convertible with a red exterior, black interior, 4-speed, and a v8 engine. After my dad and I looked it over, he gave me the shocking news. He wouldn't buy me the car because he felt that I'd get killed in it. I was devastated.

Did you know that the way I characterized this car, God thinks about us in a similar fashion? Maybe, as any car starts to put on more miles and needs repairs our impressions about it might change. However, God's thoughts about us never change.

When we were unbelievers, there's nothing about us that got Him excited. Whether someone is seven feet tall, whether they're termed a genius, whether they've invented many things, whether they're the strongest man or woman in the world, or the richest, our completeness, that's what God's looking for. This comes not from anything desirable concerning our lives but it's a spiritual quality that's received from Him at salvation. A verse from the book of Colossians tells us more about what this completeness is all about.

Colossians 2:10

> *And ye are complete in him, which is the head of all principality and power:*

Have you ever wondered what it means when Scripture says that you're *complete* in Christ?
This word in Greek can have a few meanings.
It means that in Christ:
You fully possess maximum amounts of blessings.
[You] have or share in the goodness of the nature which He is.[129]
[You're] richly furnished with the power and gifts of the Holy Spirit.[130]
[There are resources] from which [you] may be filled, that nothing may be wanting to [you].[131]

What else we know about this word in Koine Greek is that it's a verb that's classified as a perfect passive participle. Thus, we can restate this verse saying, that you received this completeness at a point in time in the past when you responded to the gospel and were placed in union with Christ and presently remain complete.

When God looks at you, He sees you continuously *complete* in His Son. And all that has been deposited in your spirit in this respect will remain no matter what. *You've been filled full, with the present result that you are in a state of [fulness, such that] in Christ [you'll] find the satisfaction of every spiritual want.*[132] So, stop looking at yourself as to what you see in the natural but start looking at yourself as always being *complete* in Him.

The next spiritual reality that has taken place in your life at salvation is a declaration that most of us have sought from family, friends, and society. Any idea what this could be referring to? Let's find out.

19

YOU ARE RIGHTEOUS

I think that most of us have sought this out in our lives from others. I only ever sought this from my father. I was, to my dismay, an only child. My mother, in her younger years, had a bad heart. After having me, she was told that she couldn't have any more children. From what I was told, she was the recipient of the second heart operation in my hometown.

As my dad exhibited uncontrollable fits of anger at times, my mother was more tempered in her approach to issues. She also liked to collect things, i.e., old records, coins, collectibles, etc. One day, when I was about seven years old, she came up to me and said, "This is yours." It was a little booklet of stamps that was the prize contained within a cereal box. When I opened it, what I saw were beautiful used US stamps. One of which was of an upside-down airplane. This began what was to become years later a large collection of US and world stamps, about twenty books.

Besides this, I began collecting baseball cards, coins, and comic books. My dad was not too thrilled with this. He thought that these hobbies were a waste of time and money.

Another thing that I enjoyed as a kid was sports. My dad, being the oldest of seven siblings, was forced at a very young age to work and help provide for his immediate family. Engaging in sports were a foreign concept to him.

While I admit that my father worked and provided food and shelter for the family, I didn't enjoy his company. We had very little in common. It seemed that no matter what I did, I sought one thing from him, as I'm sure many of us have desired from others, but to no avail.

When I entered high school, then college, and ultimately the world of work, I continually sought this one thing until one day I found someone, or instead, He found me, that provided what I'd longed for all of my life. What was it, you ask? Please turn in your Bibles to the book of 2 Corinthians.

2 Corinthians 5:21

> *For he hath made him to be sin for us, who knew no sin; that we might be made the righteousness of God in him.*

God the Father has *made him* (Christ) *to be sin*, a sin offering, a sacrifice for sin for us, who bore the punishment due to them, suffering in our stead so that *we might be made the righteousness of God in him* (in union with Christ by faith). What does it mean that we've been *made the righteousness of God in him*?

Being made righteous has many meanings. And here they are.

Christ's *righteousness* is imparted to you in the sense of His having fulfilled all the righteousness of the law for us as our representative.[133] It signifies here the salvation of God, as comprehending justification through the blood of [Christ] and sanctification through his Spirit.[134] [We're] made righteous in the sight of God; that is, [we're accepted as righteous] and treated as righteous by God on account of what the Lord Jesus has done.[135]

There it is. Do you understand what I was searching for? If you still don't know, I have one more definition of what it means to be *made the righteousness of God in Christ. The righteousness of God is taken here to denote — not that which is given [to] us by God, but that which is approved of by him.*[136]

What I sought was approval. *God is now my ardent supporter as He is yours.* At salvation, He's placed within you, i.e., in your spirit, all of which He supports, which will help you fulfill the spiritual journey that He has set before you. Give praise and thanks to God.

Have you ever had the desire to want to own something since you were a little kid? Did this ever come true? Did you know that there's one desire that holds true for God? What is it, you ask? It's waiting for you to discover it in what follows.

20

YOU ARE A PECULIAR PERSON

Is there something you own that you cherish? A dog, a cat, a baseball card, a car, a piece of jewelry, a work of art, a stamp, etc. I'm sure each of us owns something special, whether of monetary value or not. And I'll bet there's at least one thing that we wish we could own.

In the article that follows, there's something that someone wanted to buy when he was a kid but was unable to afford until he got older and had enough money to purchase it. Any idea what this was? The following article will tell us what this item was.

A $180K POKÉMON CARD AND THE GEEKIEST STUFF THAT COULD MAKE YOU RICH

Although there are many avenues you can take to earn $1 million, here's one that might surprise you: cashing in on your geeky collectibles. It sounds a little far-fetched, but some collectibles have made their [owner's] big bucks at auctions.

Just this month, a rare Pokemon card featuring the ever-popular Charizard sold for $183,812 at auction, Cardhop reported. That's the highest known price paid for this particular card. And the buyer is just as [surprised] as the price — the vintage trading card was bought by the rapper Logic.

"When I was a [kid,] I absolutely loved Pokémon but couldn't afford the cards," he wrote on Instagram. "I remember even trying to trade food stamps for [them, and now, as an adult who has saved every penny, he has made,] being able to enjoy something that I've loved since childhood now as a grown man is like buying back a piece of something I could never [have. It's not about the material,] it's about the experience."

Of course, how much your geeky collectibles are worth can be subjective and might depend on a variety of factors like condition, rarity, [age,] and demand. You'll likely need multiple rare and valuable collectibles to fetch [one] million, but it could be worth a try if you've got a collection.[137]

What we're going to take a look at is what God considers the most valuable collection in the world. Any idea what this is? Where this is found in the Bible is in the book of 1 Peter.

1 Peter 2:9

> *But ye are a chosen generation, a royal priesthood, an holy nation, a peculiar people; that ye should shew forth the praises of him who hath called you out of darkness into his marvellous light:*

The Apostle Peter was addressing Jewish and Gentile Christians who've been scattered about in different countries, telling them that collectively they're *a chosen generation* (an elect race; to all who believed in Christ), *a royal priesthood* (a body of priest-kings[138]), *a holy nation* (a multitude of people of the same nature[139]), and *a peculiar people*. What does it mean when God describes these believers as being *peculiar*? There are two meanings of the word *peculiar*, according to Thesaurus.com, which are distinct or unique. With that said, we can say that the Christian body or church is a distinct or unique people and is God's most valuable collection. *You, as a member of this body, are one of God's most valuable collections.*

But wait, there's one more perspective about these words that's taken from Wuest's Word Studies. Are you ready for it? *The phrase peculiar people refers to the unique, private, personal ownership of the saints by God. Therefore, each believer, and that includes you, is God's unique possession just as if that saint were the only human being in existence.*[140] Wow! Reflect upon that.

From this, we can deduct from the following verse what it is that God desires the most.

2 Peter 3:9c ... that all should come to repentance.

The spiritual blessing that we'll take a look at next has to do with something that I remember being taught repeatedly in the Catholic high school I attended and the church that I was brought up in. It was paramount in that what was conveyed should be obeyed under all costs. Any idea what I'm talking about? Think of Moses and the number ten.

21

YOU ARE DEAD TO THE LAW

For some of us, in our early years, the church we attended stressed obeying what is called the ten commandments. Do you remember every one of them? I don't. Well, here they are from the book of Exodus 20:3-8.

Thou shalt have no other gods before me.
Thou shalt not make unto thee any graven image, or any likeness of any thing that is in heaven above, or that is in the earth beneath, or that is in the water under the earth:
Thou shalt not take the name of the Lord thy God in vain; for the Lord will not hold him guiltless that taketh his name in vain.
Remember the sabbath day, to keep it holy.
Honour thy father and thy mother: that thy days may be long upon the land which the Lord thy God giveth thee.
Thou shalt not kill.
Thou shalt not commit adultery.
Thou shalt not steal.
Thou shalt not bear false witness against thy neighbour.
Thou shalt not covet thy neighbour's house, thou shalt not covet thy

neighbour's wife, nor his manservant, nor his maidservant, nor his ox, nor his ass, nor any thing that is thy neighbour's.

So, you tried as best you could to obey them. And if you were successful, you were probably characterized as someone who was living a moral, godly life. Right? As for myself, when I reached my late teenage years and started hanging around with a peer group that didn't go to church but rather enjoyed the pleasures of sin, it's not surprising that I stopped going. I got involved as we've heard others quote this line, with sex, drugs, and rock n roll. By my mid-twenties, my life was out of control. I didn't like anything about it.

As I mentioned earlier in this study, and will briefly, here again, I decided to attend the various faiths in my home town, hoping to find a God that would work with me in changing my life. What I found out was that most churches emphasized learning about the doctrines of their faith and the need to stop sinning. Certain sins were considered more egregious than others. I tried this approach, hoping that I'd draw closer to God, but He was nowhere to be found.

I kept on attending different faiths until one of them presented the gospel of grace to me. I responded to it and was immersed in God's love, peace, and joy. Thoughts of sinning were gone, at least for a short period of time. While sinful desires did come back, I began to learn how to address them.

What I learned was that it wasn't by obeying a command of the Mosaic Law that addressed my sinful tendencies. Even if I tried as hard as I could to stop doing this or that, this didn't stop the sinful thoughts from coming back again and again and imprisoning me once more. But I was set free by changing my thoughts concerning whatever sinful area it was that was trying to resurface and urge me to engage in it again. Let me give you one example of what I mean.

What if you're attracted to a fellow believer and begin entertaining thoughts of desiring to have a sexual relationship with them. How could this be addressed?

> *1 John 1:9 If we confess our sins, he is faithful and just to forgive us our sins, and to cleanse us from all unrighteousness.*

New Testament Scripture says that we should *confess* known sin (mental, verbal, or overt) to God the Father. Under the Law of the Old Testament, we'd simply try not to commit this sin according to one of the commandments. But, in the New Testament addressing our thoughts is of paramount importance. What we need to do next is recall Scripture and reflect upon it that provides us with what our spiritual perspective should be in this area. A verse from the book of 1 Peter will enlighten us in this regard.

> *1 Peter 1:22 Seeing ye have purified your souls in obeying the truth through the Spirit unto unfeigned love of the brethren, see that ye love one another with a pure heart fervently:*

We're instructed to *love one another with a pure heart*. The word *pure* means not for the love of ourselves or to not use for our advantage. And the word *heart* means mind. Next, I'd recommend rewriting this verse, memorizing it, and applying it when needed.

> *1 Peter 1:22b ... see that ye love one another with a pure (not for the love of ourselves; to not use for our advantage) heart (mind) fervently:*

What we're learning to do is think how God would have us think, which is according to His illumination of such in the Epistles. And guess what amazing thing happens? The book of 1 John will tell us so.

> *1 John 2:5 But whoso keepeth his word, in him verily is the love of God perfected: hereby know we that we are in him.*

As we choose to continually keep God's *word* (all that he has made known to us as His will in regard to our conduct), *the love of God* (love produced in us by the Holy Spirit) will be *perfected* (manifested; an experiential realization of divine affection; characterized, not by any representative trait or quality of [our personality], but merely as the subject of the work of divine love.[141]

We're no longer trying to obey an Old Testament command but confess sin and change how we think under a new dispensation of thought. When we do this, the passions of the sin nature that would continue to reign under the Law will be replaced with the fruit or influences of the Holy Spirit. And as such, our thoughts and thus our responses toward fellow believers and unbelievers will be Christ-centered.

So, what does the Word of God say is the relationship between Christians and the Mosaic Law? Please go to the book of Romans.

> *Romans 7:4 Wherefore, my brethren, ye also are become dead to the law by the body of Christ; that ye should be married to another, even to him who is raised from the dead, that we should bring forth fruit unto God.*

It says that you are *dead to the law* at salvation. You are completely delivered from its authority as a covenant of works, and more especially from its power to condemn[142] because of Christ's death on the cross. *It's no longer the regulatory system for spiritual growth.* Does it have any usefulness? Yes, the Law still has its place, but not for us. If not for us, then who? A verse from the book of 1 Timothy will tell us so.

> *1 Timothy 1:8-9 But we know that the law is good, if a man use it lawfully; Knowing this, that the law is not made for a righteous man, but for the lawless and disobedient, for the ungodly and for sinners, for unholy and profane, for murderers of fathers and murderers of mothers, for manslayers,*

The law is good (morally excellent), *if a man use it lawfully* (as it should be used). This begs the question; how should it be used? The Law is designed to show people their sinfulness. [Thus,] the Law is not for one who had already recognized his sin and turned to Christ. That person is no longer under the Law but should now walk in the Spirit ([Galatians] 5:13-26). *The Law is intended for those who remain unconvinced of their sin.*[143]

So, remember, you're dead to the law, i.e., like a widow released from marital obligations, so [you're] released from the Law and its arousal to sin. The purpose of this release "from the Law" is so that [you] may [serve in] the new way of the Spirit, and not in the old way of the written code.[144]

The spiritual blessing that we'll take a look at next has to do with superpowers. Have you ever wanted to be a superhero? Did you know that you are one of them because you possess something that makes you such? Would you like to know what that is? You know the drill. Please turn the page.

22

YOU ARE A POSSESSOR OF ETERNAL LIFE

When I was a young boy, I collected comic books. Each month, when the new ones would come out, my mother would take me to a store called Woolworths. They had a separate comic book section that I couldn't wait to see. I'd try to find only those that were first edition or #1 issue amongst hundreds of different ones. And then I'd sheepishly ask her if she'd buy them for me.

Over time, I had the #1 first issue of Spiderman, the X-Men, the Fantastic Four, and the Green Hornet. While I also liked Superman and Batman comics, the #1 issues were produced many years earlier and were unaffordable. Was there one that was my favorite? I'd have to say Spiderman. Why was this the case? It had to do with who he was, what his superpowers were, how he got them, and what his mission was. These answers were found from the following information provided by Wikipedia.

SPIDER-MAN

Spider-Man is the alias of Peter Parker, an orphan raised by his Aunt May and [uncle in New York City after his parents, Richard and Mary Parker,] died in a plane crash ... Spider-Man gets superhuman spider-powers and abilities from a bite from a radioactive spider; these include clinging to surfaces and ceilings, superhuman strength, speed, and agility, and detecting danger with his precognition ability called "spider-sense." He also builds wrist-mounted "web-shooter" devices that shoot artificial spider-webs of his own design that was meant to be used for shooting and trapping his enemies and web-swinging across the city. After the personal tragedy of his late Uncle Ben, Peter began using his spider-powers to fight against crime as Spider-Man.[145]

My favorite superpower of his was the ability to web-swing across the city. I liken it to being able to fly. Do you know that you've received at salvation a supernatural blessing that contains supernatural powers? The book of 1 John will fill us in as to what you've acquired.

1 John 5:11

And this is the record, that God hath given to us eternal life, and this life is in his Son.

And this is the testimony that *God* the Father has given you *eternal life* when you chose to believe *in his Son*. With that said, what is *eternal life*? It's that life in God that includes all [blessedness and isn't] broken by physical death.[146] *We can also describe it as the zoe or divine life.* Another aspect of eternal life is brought forth in the following verse.

1 John 5:12

He that hath the Son hath life; and he that hath not the Son of God hath not life.

The phrase *hath life* tells us that every believer is in full and continuous possession of[147] it. Your new life continues in the now and forever. You can't escape it. You can't lose it. *And what comes with divine life are many blessings, one of which is called spiritual gifts or divine empowerments, which are, in actuality, supernatural powers.* By means of the agency of the indwelling Spirit, He directs us to use whatever gift of gifts He has given us for the edification of the church and an awareness of the existence of God for unbelievers.

Let me give you one example of these gifts and how it functions. One of them is called the gift of knowledge (1 Corinthians 12:8). This benefit is the revealing of a fact in existence (of the present or past) that can only be supernaturally revealed. In other words, this [isn't] something that could be known naturally but something one's eyes [haven't seen] and ears [haven't] heard.[148]

And besides this, it's possible that each of us will receive additional powers when we pass on from here, enter heaven, and receive glorified bodies. Some examples of this pertain to the time when Jesus was witnessed by over five hundred people during a period of 40 days on the earth after He rose from the dead.

> *John 20:19 Then the same day at evening, being the first day of the week, when the doors were shut where the disciples were assembled for fear of the Jews, came Jesus and stood in the midst, and saith unto them, Peace be unto you.*

The word *shut* can also mean locked. Could this indicate that Jesus actually passed through the door with supernatural ability?

> *Acts 1:9 And when he had spoken these things, while they beheld, he was taken up; and a cloud received him out of their sight.*

This was the time when Jesus departed from the earth toward heaven. It appears that He was flying.

> *Revelations 19:14 And the armies which were in heaven followed him upon white horses, clothed in fine linen, white and clean.*

And as for us, Jesus' bride, we're told that there will come a time in the future when we'll return with Him on white horses, accompanying Him at His return to the earth. On flying horses in outer space? I know what you're thinking. All of this is a figure of speech. Well, if it isn't, then there could be many Spider-men and Spider-women in heaven. Ha-ha.

With that said, you have eternal or divine life and as such you're a superhero who has been provided with supernatural powers. This means that you're exceptional. Think about that.

The next spiritual reality that has taken place in your life at salvation is a designation that describes you as someone who represents someone else. Any idea what the name of this position is?

23

YOU ARE AN AMBASSADOR

Any idea what the qualifications are for someone who desires to be an ambassador for the United States? The article that we'll take a look at next will tell us what an ambassador does and how someone can become one.

HOW TO BECOME A US AMBASSADOR

The need for efficient, progressive diplomatic relationships between nations is of the utmost importance. *Ambassadors either have a career as Foreign Service Officers (FSOs) or are non-career political appointees.* The fact that this title is prestigious and comes with a great amount of responsibility means it also requires individuals who live up to the title, stand out from the crowd, and have established professional experience. So, what does it take to become a U.S. ambassador?

What Do U.S. Ambassadors Do?

Ambassadors represent the U.S. government, or their country of origin, in place of the president or a leader. Ambassadors are also known as diplomats, as a more general term. These professionals also help travelers from their home country, explain foreign policy, and evacuate refugees from dangerous situations. Due to their careers' delicate nature, ambassadors conduct their duties with a diplomatic mindset, intending to maintain a positive relationship between countries.

Further on, [we'll] discuss what steps to follow if you aspire to become a U.S. ambassador.

EDUCATION AND REQUIREMENTS

Ambassadors must have stellar verbal and written communication skills. In diplomatic circles, a keen knowledge of current events—both domestic and international—is crucial. As early as you can, keep up to date with worldwide news and engage about political issues. If opportunities exist, attend publicly accessible seminars by visiting diplomats or government officials and conferences on foreign policy matters.

What to [Study to Become] an Ambassador?

Even though [the] educational requirements to become an ambassador are not specific, like with many specialist positions, a graduate degree is preferred or required with the Foreign Service. Most ambassadors hold a degree in political science, international relations, history, or other related disciplines. A master's degree or Ph.D. can accelerate the diplomatic career of aspiring ambassadors. Also, these individuals tend to include foreign language courses in their studies.

What [Will Make You Stand Out]?

Certain things will make you stand out from other potential Foreign Service candidates. Being fluent in other languages is a high-demand quality. Some languages include Mandarin, Arabic, Farsi, and Turkish.

From early on, prospective ambassadors should:

- Develop leadership skills
- Lay the foundation for political affiliation
- Do as much humanitarian work as possible

Internships and overseas experience are fundamental for this career path. The U.S. Department of State offers two internship paths for students interested in U.S. foreign policy and diplomacy:

- The Pathways Internship Program
- The U.S. Department of State Student Internship Program

Other worthwhile and valuable internships and volunteer opportunities include organizations such as:

- The United Nations
- UNESCO (United Nations Educational, Scientific, and Cultural Organization)
- The World Bank
- The International Organization for Migration
- The Peace Corps

Personal [Qualities]
Essentially, the ambassador's job is to be a mediator between two governments, which are often not likely to agree on all issues. The role, while highly regarded, is demanding to a fault. Some indispensable qualities include:

- The capacity to stay poised, to think on one's feet, and to maintain self-control
- Be adaptive, value systems, political beliefs, and economic circumstances of other cultures

- Have the ability to absorb complex information from various sources and draw rational conclusions
- The capability to discern what is appropriate, practical, and sensible in a given situation
- Have [the] quality to stay unbiased to avoid deceit, favoritism, and discrimination
- The potential to establish positive relationships and gain the confidence of others

CAREER GROWTH

This isn't a job you can [obtain] overnight. You have to climb up the ladder by showing potential and determination. Here are steps that you should follow to be eligible for an ambassadorship.

Choose a [Profession]

To become a U.S. ambassador, firstly, you need to become a Foreign Service Officer. Selecting a career track is a major decision since you may not be able to change your mind once you choose a path during the registration for the Foreign Service Officer Test (FSOT). Career opportunities include:

- Consular Officer
- Economic Officer
- Management Officer
- Political Officer
- Public Diplomacy Officer

The Foreign Service Officer Test (FSOT)

After deciding on a career, you can register for the tests before deadlines or until capacity is reached. Before taking the Foreign

Service Officer Test, you may take the FSOT Practice Test to experience a practical preview and receive an estimate of your likelihood of passing the FSOT.

If you pass the FSOT multiple-choice section, you will receive an email asking you to submit a Personal Narrative (PN) to the Qualifications Evaluation Panel (QEP). Successful applicants then get invited to take the Oral Assessment. If you successfully pass the Foreign Service Officer Test, Qualifications Evaluation Panel, Oral Assessment, security and medical clearances, and a suitability review, [you're] placed on a hiring register. People with higher scores will be positioned higher and hired depending on the needs of the Foreign Service.

Gain [Experience]

Part of life in the Foreign Service is moving every few years. Even if [they're] not in your primary focus area or are located in distant or precarious locations, accept all posts submitted to you. This way, by being flexible, you prove your commitment to the career of diplomacy and your ambition to be groomed for an ambassadorship.

Once you get your first job, you'll need to work your way up, so make sure to be noticeable, do your job well, and network. As much as skills are important, networking plays a big part in reaching your final goal. Become an expert on the history, geography, culture, language, political systems, and role of that particular country in the global economy.

Receive Appointment

Climbing the ladder, as mentioned before, requires time and continuous commitment. By getting involved with your chosen political party and showing [reliability] and attentiveness, the odds are more in your favor at attracting national attention from decision-makers.

Overall, engage as much as possible with the U.S. government's policy on that country. Hopefully, [you'll get nominated as ambassador by the president] to serve as a United States diplomat to individual nations of the world, international organizations, or ambassador-at-large.

Gaining ambassadorship is a process that will take unmatched dedication, time, and an impressive skill set. However, if you put both your mind and heart [into] it, the journey will be well worth it. We hope these tips helped guide you. Additionally, if you were unsure about following this path, and this article convinced you, you can start by enrolling in BAU's Bachelor of Arts in Political Science and International Relations program.[149]

As we've become aware, becoming a US ambassador takes years of effort. Well, what about you? Are you an ambassador? For whom? A verse from the book of 2 Corinthians will provide us with the answer.

2 Corinthians 5:20

> *Now then we are ambassadors for Christ, as though God did beseech you by us: we pray you in Christ's stead, be ye reconciled to God.*

Did you know that you're an ambassador *for Christ*, i.e., someone who represents and carries a message from Him to be presented to those who don't know Him personally? As God did *beseech* (plead; appeal to) the Corinthians by the Apostle Paul and Timothy, before they were saved, to respond to the gospel of repentance and faith, likewise, they prayed after their conversion that they would also engage in and present this same message to those that weren't saved, i.e., so that they may become *reconciled to God*.

Whether the Corinthian saints responded to the encouragement to share the good news of Christ, they're still ambassadors for Him. And so are you. Their response didn't change their position before God.

Whether you might consider yourself as someone who can't witness to others because you have issues, this doesn't change the criteria that has made you Christ's ambassador. What are they, you ask? You are: accepted in the beloved, sealed with the Holy Spirit, beloved, a new creation, complete in Christ, etc.

Don't allow the way you've been thinking, speaking, or acting cast doubt on whether you're truly someone who represents Christ. *Remember, you're an ambassador who acts on Christ's behalf, whose duty is to publish the tidings of redemption, the offer of pardon, [and to urge and entreat] men that they accept the gospel and thus enjoy the blessings of reconciliation with God.* - T.[150] So, learn and reflect upon God's Word one day, one hour, one moment at a time on whom God says you are. And over time, this verse will become a reality in your life.

> *Isaiah 55:11 So shall my word be that goeth forth out of my mouth: it shall not return unto me void, but it shall accomplish that which I please, and it shall prosper in the thing whereto I sent it.*

One of the most misunderstood blessings that you've inherited is what we'll take a look at next. Any idea what this might pertain to in regard to your new life in Christ? Let's find out.

24

YOU ARE GOD'S WORKMANSHIP

Have you ever heard of the word 'masterpiece?' What comes to your mind when you hear this word? For me, what I think of are works of art that are one of a kind and are considered pinnacle examples of the painting art world. From my understanding, there are different kinds of painting artwork, such as realism, expressionism, abstract, pop, etc.? Do you have a favorite? I do.

I don't know why but I've always been enamored with realism, i.e., a style that is a reflection of the real world. I like scenes of the countryside. Landscape gives you a glimpse into what these places looked like at that time. Do you have any idea what the name is of the most famous realism painting? Do you know who painted it? I have an article ready for you to read that will tell us about it.

A BRIEF HISTORY OF THE MONA LISA, THE WORLD'S MOST FAMOUS PAINTING

Leonardo da Vinci's iconic *Mona Lisa*, the world's most famous, recognizable, and copied artwork, has a storied history. Painted between 1503 and 1519, it was owned by French royalty for centuries. Liberated by Revolutionary forces, the painting briefly adorned Napoleon's bedroom, then was installed in the Louvre. Over 80% of Louvre visitors come specifically to see *Mona Lisa*. Due to new queuing practices, visitors have only [thirty] seconds to admire the painting's legendary mystique.

Thought by most scholars to be a portrait of Italian noble Lisa del Giocondo, this beautiful, dark-haired woman with an enigmatic gaze has fascinated people for ages. Unlike most 16th-century portraits of nobility, which showed off their social status and wealth with flamboyant clothing, [hairstyles,] and accessories, Mona Lisa is dressed in elegant simplicity, which draws attention to her face.

Painted in a revolutionary ¾ length pose—contrary to typical Italian portraiture, which used full figure poses—Mona Lisa is not stoic or demure. Deviating from traditional female portraiture, she meets our eyes directly, as a man typically would, turning slightly [toward] the viewer, smiling at some secret amusement. Da Vinci's expert portrayal of a subtle smile illustrates [an] exhaustive understanding of human anatomy, while his deliberately irregular brushstrokes over her face give the skin a realistic texture.

Mona Lisa showcases many painterly techniques da Vinci employed, including sfumato and aerial perspective. DaVinci used sfumato, which means ["vanished" or "evaporated,"] to create imperceptible transitions between light and [dark] while the background fades into the distance. This is another deviation from traditional Italian portraiture, which painted the background [with] the same sharp focus as the central figure.

Relatively unknown to the general [public] but lauded as a masterwork by artists and intelligentsia, *Mona Lisa*'s 1911 theft brought notoriety. Picasso, French poet Apollinaire and American tycoon JP Morgan were all suspects during the investigation, but the actual culprit was Louvre employee Vincenzo Peruggia, with two accomplices. One of the accomplices claimed to have made six indistinguishable forgeries, leading to a rumor that the Mona Lisa currently in the Louvre is a fake.

Now exhibited in a [climate-controlled] case made of bulletproof glass, *Mona Lisa* has survived vandalism and attempted theft. Moved into a glass case sometime in the [1950s], because an obsessive fan tried to cut it out with a razor blade and take it [home; the painting was slightly damaged in 1956] when a thrown rock shattered the glass case, dislodging a speck of pigment near her left elbow. The newer bulletproof case has continued to protect it. In 1974, while on loan for an exhibition at [the Tokyo] Museum, the painting was sprayed with red paint by an activist protesting [the] lack of disability access. Back at the Louvre, in 2009, a woman threw a teacup at it because she'd been denied French citizenship.

[Also,] one of the most expensive paintings in the world, *Mona Lisa* became a Guinness World Records holder in 1962 for the highest known painting insurance valuation, $100 million, which is at least $870 million today. Given that it's deemed irreplaceable, it's probably worth more.[151]

Did you know that many are unaware that there's another masterpiece that's the greatest of all masterpieces? Who is it of? And who made it? The book of Ephesians will tell us so.

Ephesians 2:10

> *For we are his workmanship, created in Christ Jesus unto good works, which God hath before ordained that we should walk in them.*

You're God's *workmanship* (his work of art or a masterpiece[152]), *created* (made a new spiritual creature) *in Christ Jesus*. For what purpose? To perform *good works*. The believer has God working in him, and therefore his works are good. His works are not good because [he's] good, but because he has a new nature from God, and because the Holy Spirit works in him and through him to produce these good works.[153]

Now you know who the most incredible masterpiece is. It's you. You're God's saving work, i.e., a new spiritual creation in Christ Jesus. Nothing can compare to you. Your value is beyond measure.

Do you know that you've been blessed with an assurance of where you'll reside when life passes you on? Let's found out more about this.

25

YOU ARE RESURRECTED AND SEATED TOGETHER WITH CHRIST

For some, life is no longer worth living. The reasons are varied. All of us are only here for a short period of time, and yet when we hear reports of someone taking their own life, we wonder what could have caused such a paramount decision. Contained here is an article about such.

MICHELLE'S STORY

[It's not about being brave in sharing; it's] about being real and hoping to end the widely stigmatized thoughts regarding an illness.

Mental illness, the vast array of judged, [shunned,] and misunderstood group of stigmatized illnesses. Suicide, the part of mental illness [that's even more judged, misunderstood,] and stigmatized. The people and families who deal with mental illness need to feel safe to get help and to discuss [what's considered taboo subjects in order for acceptance, so they don't] fear asking for help. [It's possible in time to have healthy, open dialogue about these subjects, and it's] time the world learns how. It is a [life,] or death situation. There are many organizations dedicated to educating and creating [awareness;] please research them.

I suffer from mental illness and all of its ugly, painful effects. My hope is to inspire others to come out and share their stories without fear and to inspire others to educate themselves and try to understand. This [isn't] my way of trying to get sympathy or play [the] victim. This is the most real I can be in summing up a lifetime of [pain] about a subject that needs to be discussed openly and publicly in order to save lives and end stigma.

I suffer from major depression that [doesn't stem from situational circumstances,] and I have suicidal tendencies. Not to say some [life-changing situations didn't affect my depression, but for the most part, it's] biological. As it stands now in society, mental illness becomes a label, a directive of how some people may judge [you] before even meeting you or knowing anything else about you. Some people resist treatment [because they're scared that an employer, school, doctor, or other important life guides] may deny or judge them.

Many people [don't] understand how to deal with a depressed friend or relative or acquaintance. [It's easier to pretend it doesn't] exist, title them as the crazy one, or say things that actually minimize the disease, that [suggests] it will just magically go away. Ex: just work out, eat healthier, do yoga, snap out of it. The cycle [begins;] nobody feels comfortable hearing about depression or [suicide,] and then the depressed individual hides their pain, fearing judgment, [embarrassment,] or being labeled.

[I've] dealt with depression since childhood; it took years for me to understand what it was and why I was different. I fought [it for years;] I never gave up. Many never knew I struggled. From the exterior [I've been perceived as outgoing, approachable, and fun; it wasn't] a facade, as my personality [isn't] my depression. It has even gone so far as overhearing a psychiatric nurse say, "[She's so pretty;] how can she be depressed?" The way I look is not my depression.

My junior year of college was my first suicide attempt. [I'd] classify it as a cry for help, not a true attempt. I had no [plan. My roommates were home, and I was intoxicated. I didn't just want attention;] I needed it. I went into the bathroom with a [razor, and when my roommates broke into the room,] I cried in relief.

My mom drove out, picked me [up,] and put me right into intense therapy. I had also been suffering from bulimia since age [fifteen which] had been escalating while away at school. I turned to working through my eating disorder, not realizing at the time that it was all related. I was always doing anything to escape the pain of my emotions. From that point forward, I had this deep nagging voice inside that told me suicide would ultimately be my demise if I ever got over the fear of the [act. Thankfully] I was always too scared as I still had hope.

Fast forward, after years of medication trials, different types of [therapy,] and reaching a point where the side effects of medications outweighed the problems they were prescribed [for, my life became a] slew of side effects and more medications to treat the side effects. Those of us with mental illness like to refer to these as "med cocktails." I started to [get tired of all the doctors, therapy appointments, and side effects] while still struggling with low moods regularly. The day Amy Winehouse [died, I was watching the news coverage,] and all I could think of was how lucky she was that she was finally out of her pain. Impulsively, I took an overdose of sleeping pills and benzodiazepines. I sent a few "I love you [texts,]" and someone who knew of my struggles and had family experience with suicide took that random text as a hint and called [the] police to do a wellness check on me. I was taken to the ER. It turned out I [didn't take enough pills to do the job;] the ER actually let me leave.

A month [later, I sunk even lower and] I gave up. I was done fighting [the] inner demons that tried to hold me down and hold me back. I was so tired of fighting. I felt I was a burden and saw no other way out of the pain. It was not [selfishness. In my mind,] it was truly the answer to alleviate my pain and the pain I burdened others with. I wrote a suicide [note, surrounded myself with photos of people I love,] and took a much more intense overdose. I lay next to my cat, crying that he would never see me awake again.

I attempted suicide. There was no turning back from that act. I sent one friend an "I love you" text once the drugs had reached a point of [intoxication,] and I passed out. He had learned from my [previous] attempt what to do. He called the police. My doorman knew me well and [witnessed] my first attempt and let the police in. Thirteen days later, [two on a medical floor and eleven] on a locked psychiatric ward, four years later, countless therapy [sessions, and I still haven't] fully recovered. My depression actually got worse and was combined with shame, [fear, and embarrassment that created a deep,] oozing wound that never [seemed to fully heal. It's] hard to look in the mirror daily knowing that the person staring back at me tried to kill me. Imagine that.

Look beyond for a moment from the pain it causes loved ones, but the pain it causes to oneself when [you've] already suffered most of your life. Knowing that you woke up when you wanted to die and now need to rebuild your own belief system [regarding] yourself. Rebuild the ability for others to trust you not to repeat your actions; try to protect the hearts of loved ones. Rebuild the strength to fight the unending battle yet again. While feeling like Bambi and feeling like you have to hide what you did.

I googled "help for suicide [survivors," and] all that came up was help for the loved ones that survived someone who had [completed suicide] and how to help them cope. I [couldn't believe it. I was a survivor; I survived self-murder; I was the one left like a newborn] with open raw wounds and wanted the help of others like me. I found nothing. Thankfully in just the four years since my attempts, this is changing. People are starting to come [forward; organizations are realizing the importance and it's changing. I'm slowly reaching out to them, and they're giving me the] courage and strength I never knew I had. That is such a huge step forward.

I believe that suicidal thoughts and suicidal actions are different. I believe that once you cross that line into [action, it actually becomes an option in the future, that it's] never truly safe to have the thoughts again without having a safe support system to openly express the thoughts in a nonjudgmental way. The actions become an [answer,] and the thoughts can evolve into action. Thoughts are thoughts. [Actions,] however can change the world. Change life.

This is why [it's] so important to open up dialogue publicly about suicide and mental illness. The statistics show that many completed suicides are not initial attempts. Those that need help [aren't] just those with the thoughts, but those that have already tried to end their lives. Being one of these people, I know firsthand that [there's more shame and more fear after an attempt than] when I was having just thoughts.

Surviving my attempt backfired on me and made me feel like I [didn't want to overutilize my long-developed support.] I had put so many loved ones through [hell, and I didn't want to seem overly needy;] I isolated myself more than ever. I put the people who supported me through so much that I feared letting them know I was still struggling to heal. I wanted everyone to think I was ok, back to normal. [However, I'm] still not ok.

[I'm blessed with a strong mother who asks me daily if I'm] ok. My boss checks on me [daily. I] have a small handful of friends that know my silence is a queue to call and check on me. Sadly, many of my friends and family do nothing unless I bring it up, which [isn't easy when I don't] know how they feel about it.

Once the shock and initial responses occur, life for others tends to go back to normal. Many have no idea how to behave or what to believe. Some think it was just a moment of bad [judgment. They don't understand that it's] an ongoing illness and just because you survived, [doesn't] mean the illness disappears. This is the ideal time for family and friends to take time to educate [themselves] instead of going back to acting like it never happened. Yes, some suicides are [impulsive, and due to circumstances, and] this is also where education is so helpful.

When discussing my intentions of openly discussing my suicidal tendencies with a few people in my support system, I was met with positive [reactions,] until the questions were asked. You [don't] mean posting it on social media or putting the information somewhere

[where] total strangers could see this right? This [isn't going to be shared with people you know,] right?

Wow! Had the past several years of my discussion of how important it is to take away the stigma gone unheard? When I said publicly, I meant publicly, not partially [public,] except for those that may judge me. It saddened me to hear that the very people I rely on, even if for that moment in [the] conversation, judged my decision to share such personal details. If [I'm] to become an advocate and help others like [me,] it has to be open and real. *The most important thing anyone can do for someone expressing suicidal thoughts is to listen and not judge or minimize what [they're] saying.*

Open dialogue has to start [somewhere,] and my somewhere starts now. [I'm still a good person. I'm still kind and intelligent and reasonable. I'm] also gifted with insight, the ability to forgive, and admit [wrongdoing]. I appreciate my ability to relate to others on many levels and be open-minded. I also have [a mental illness. It doesn't define me, but it's] part of who I am.

[I'm] relieving my conscious of the secret I held due to fear of being judged or misunderstood. [I have a lifetime illness; I struggle in some way, almost daily, and it's] real. A suicide note is real. Quiet struggles are real. A beautiful smile may or may not be real. Talking openly is not just real; [it's] necessary.

Please rethink your ideas regarding mental [illness and ask those you love if they're ok. A] simple smile can change another person's day and learn the symptoms, the signs. It [isn't contagious. It is,] however deadly.

I can sum my experience up in a poem I wrote:
My silence is an echo of my repetitive pain,
Reminding me of demons that live in my brain.
They haunt my days and stir my fears,
They have been there living for all my years.
Some days are bright, some weeks, a month,
[Eventually, though,] they come to the front.
They scream so loud I cry in shame,
But only I can hear this pain.

My silence protects the demons from showing,
People often judge me but [they're] really unknowing.
To think that depression has a sound or first [name] is as ignorant as thinking two think the same.
If you hear nothing but [silence,] beware,
Ask before assuming the person [doesn't] care.
Silence is my prison that mimics [I'm] okay,
The demons are [there,] and I fight them every day.[154]

The least I can say about this article is that it's intense. Some might say that there's no easy fix for mental illness and recurring thoughts about committing suicide. However, I know of someone who's business it is to work deep within our lives. He gets beneath into our core nature, beliefs, desires, etc., and provides us with the help we need to be able to address any disturbing aspects of our life. And not only so, when it's our time to depart from this earth, he has also prepared a place for us where all hurts, illnesses, regrets, etc., are gone. Let's find out more about this eternal realm and how it relates to us right now. Please turn to the book of Ephesians.

Ephesians 2:6

> *And hath raised us up together, and made us sit together in heavenly places in Christ Jesus:*

God the Father had *raised up* the Ephesians' believers from spiritual death to spiritual life in *heavenly places* at a point of time in the past when they responded to the gospel. And not only so, but they were also made to *sit together* with Him. This means that while they reside on the earth, their spiritual position is in heavenly places.

Like them, you're positionally resurrected. [Your] vital union with [Christ] is the ground of [your] present spiritual and future bodily resurrection and ascension.[155] *Conversely, you have assigned to both your body and spirit a place seated together with Christ in heaven, which in due time you'll take possession of.* And as you learn how to set your heart on things above, you'll get a glimpse of what's waiting for you when you get to heaven.

If you're someone who's having difficulty living your life whether caused by biological, circumstances, abuse, addictions, etc., there's someone who wants to help you. You see, there's a God, a personal God who can change you from the inside out and help you learn how to be an overcomer no matter what difficulty you're facing. Take a look at some of the verses of Scripture contained below that clearly reveal God's heart and how He can help those who come to Him.

> *Psalms 147:3 He healeth the broken in heart, and bindeth up their wounds.*

The Lord *healeth* (makes healthful) *the broken in heart* (miserable heart), *and bindeth up* (cures; bestows peace; comforts) *their wounds* (mental sorrows; griefs and troubles).

> Psalms 107:9 For he satisfieth the longing soul, and filleth the hungry soul with goodness.

God *satisfieth* (makes provision for the needs of) *the longing* (thirsty) *soul.* He also *filleth the hungry soul with goodness* (that which imparts strength and happiness).[156]

> *Matthew 11:28-29*
> *28 Come unto me, all ye that labour and are heavy laden, and I will give you rest.*

Believe in me, you that *labour* (work) and are *heavy laden* (tired; weary), *and I will give you rest* (refreshment and rejuvenation).

> *29 Take my yoke upon you, and learn of me; for I am meek and lowly in heart: and ye shall find rest unto your souls.*

Take my yoke (an obligation to do a particular thing, i.e., submission to Christ) *upon you, and learn of me* (to learn the truths that He teaches). And if you do this, you'll find *rest* (relief, peace, quietness; have a proper fellowship with Me) in *your souls.*

Did you know that this God can change your life right now? He can provide you with a new nature, i.e., a divine life. He can change your desires with new ones. He can change your weaknesses and become your source of strength. He can change destructive thoughts into uplifting ones. And He can do so much more. So, what about you? Do you want to stay where you are or enter into an entirely new realm, i.e., a spiritual one? If your answer is yes, then here's your remedy. It's a confession that you can express right now. You can read it silently to yourself or out loud.

God the Father, I acknowledge that I have sinned in many areas, such as slandering others; having sexual relations outside of marriage; being jealous; having participated in alcohol or drug abuse; having sex with others of the same gender; committing adultery; taking money from others in a deceitful manner; committing rape; engaging in pedophilia; etc. I don't want to continue in these mental, verbal, and overt sins. I need a new nature.

I believe in your Son Jesus Christ as one of the members of the Trinity, who, as God pre-existed time; came to the earth and took on the form of a man, being born of a virgin (no sin nature); lived a sinless life; listened to and obeyed the directives of his Father; went to the cross and paid for the penalty of and forgave the sins of the whole world; rose from the dead after three days, never to die again, walked the earth in His resurrection body for forty days witnessing to over five hundred people and ascended into heaven to be seated at the right hand of God the Father.

And according to your promise, send the Holy Spirit to come and indwell my body, thus imparting to me a new nature along with all of the additional benefits promised.

Thank you!

. . .

Now, one of the members of the Trinity, the Holy Spirit, has come to indwell your body. He will serve as your counselor, guide, teacher, comforter, etc. You have become a new creation. Over time, He'll give you glimpses of His working in your life. Ask Him whatever it is that you need help with. He's always there for you.

Of all of the spiritual blessings that we've looked at up to now, this next one is probably the most controversial. Let's find out why.

26

YOU ARE HEALED

What comes to mind when you think of the word *healed*? I'd assume it would have something to do with physical healing, right? Did you know that there are many different meanings of this word depending on where it's used in Scripture? Let's begin by taking a look at its usage in a verse from the book of 1 Peter.

1 Peter 2:24

> *Who his own self bare our sins in his own body on the tree*
> *that we, being dead to sins, should live unto righteousness:*
> *by whose stripes ye were healed.*

What I recently found out was that the meaning of the word *healed* in this verse has caused major friction amongst the leadership in the body of Christ. Over the past six months, I started watching many of the TV broadcasts of a well-known Christian teacher. Apparently, he has come up with what he calls a ground breaking revelation of the relationship between grace and faith. After hearing what he had to say, I admit that Scripture appeared to support this analogy.

Another thing that I heard him teach about were the many truths about how God sees us positionally when we responded to the gospel. For instance, he declares that many believers try to be righteous by what they do and yet in Christ they are righteous. And after mentioning a few other spiritual realties he said something like, did you know that God also sees you as being healed?

The idea being that if a Christian gets cancer or any other debilitating illness then they should claim that they're already healed in the eyes of God and continue in this belief waiting for Him to fully restore them to full health in His timetable. And the verse that he uses to support this view is the one we're studying right now.

I just want to add this point. I have no dog in this fight. Let's study this verse and try to determine whether the word *healed* means physical healing or something else. So, where should we begin? Let's begin by translating as much of this verse as we can, and then we'll proceed from there.

Jesus *bare* (bore the punishment of) *our sins in his own body* (endured the same kind of physical pain that the guilty do who are punished for their own sins[157]) *on the tree* (cross). And those who repented and believed in Him, *being dead to sins* (being effectually separated from sin - that is, being so that it no longer influences [them])[158] *should live unto righteousness* (holiness). Then comes the confusing statement, *by whose stripes* (refers to the process of being wounded, that is to say, the suffering which is involved in such wounding[159]) *ye were healed.*

The ultimate question is, what does the verb *healed* mean? Commentators have different opinions with respect to this. The different interpretations are physical healing, the healing of an illness, spiritual healing, i.e., recovering from our faults, being made whole again, restored to spiritual health, righteous in living, or the salvation of those who believed in Christ. It's argued by many analysts vigorously that physical healing couldn't be the meaning of such because this wasn't something that Christ's atonement provided.

The confusion as to why much reasoning is flawed in this respect is because there's a lack of understanding between what Christ accomplished on the cross, i.e., redemption and forgiveness, and the blessings received when someone responds to the gospel. All I'm saying is that the word *healed* could refer to physical healing. Whether it does or not, hopefully we'll find out as we study further.

The verb *being dead* in Koine Greek is in the form of an aorist middle participle. If we were to translate this part of the verse, it could read something like this. Because Christ bore our sins in His own body on the cross, we ourselves became *dead to sins* when we believed the gospel message at a point in time.

Now, let's take a look at the verb *healed* in Koine Greek. This is in the form of an aorist passive indicative. Translating this part of the verse, it could be written something like this: Christ endured the process of suffering on the cross. And it's a fact that we were *healed*, when we believed in Him at a point in time in the past.

We're back to trying to answer the question, *healed* in what sense? The first avenue to take a look at is the context. What does this word mean in the verse that it's found in? If the meaning isn't clear, then are there verses that occur before or after it that helps us to understand what topic was being discussed? But before we do, why don't we start by using a concordance and find out where the word *healed* is found in other places in Scripture that use the same Greek verb *iaomai* and try to determine if there's only one meaning for it. If there is, then we've probably found out what it means in this verse. This verb is found in the book of 1 Peter.

> *Acts 3:11 And as the lame man which was healed held Peter and John, all the people ran together unto them in the porch that is called Solomon's, greatly wondering.*

I think it's pretty obvious that the word *healed* in this verse pertains to physical healing.

Another place this verb is found is in the book of Luke.

> *Luke 17:12, 15 And as he entered into a certain village, there met him ten men that were lepers, which stood afar off: And one of them, when he saw that he was healed, turned back, and with a loud voice glorified God,*

Again, I think it's pretty clear that the word *healed* means the healing of an illness. The next book I'd like you to turn to is the book of James.

> *James 5:14-16 Is any sick among you? let him call for the elders of the church; and let them pray over him, anointing him with oil in the name of the Lord: And the prayer of faith shall save the sick, and the Lord shall raise him up; and if he have committed sins, they shall be forgiven him. Confess your faults one to another, and pray one for another, that ye may be healed. The effectual fervent prayer of a righteous man availeth much.*

What this conveys to us is that if a believer is physically sick, then they should call for the pastors of the church to pray over them and anoint the forehead with oil so that they might be *healed*. If, during this intervention, there's brought to remembrance in the believer's mind an incident where they sinned against a fellow Christian, then they should go to them privately and admit guilt, which wouldn't only bring about reconciliation but the removal of the sickness. In this sense, it appears that the word healed refers to both the restoration of spiritual health and physical healing.

Another meaning that some commentators suggest that the word *healed* means is the salvation of those who believed in Christ. I couldn't find any verses that supported this rendering unless if the one we're about to look at in context affirms it.

As we can see, there are at least two different meanings for the word *healed* depending on its usage in Scripture. Keeping these in the back of our mind, let's take a look at the verses that come before or after 1 Peter 2:24 and try and determine what was being discussed.

> *1 Peter 2:18-20 Servants, be subject to your masters with all fear; not only to the good and gentle, but also to the froward. For this is thankworthy, if a man for conscience toward God endure grief, suffering wrongfully. For what glory is it, if, when ye be buffeted for your faults, ye shall take it patiently? but if, when ye do well, and suffer for it, ye take it patiently, this is acceptable with God.*
>
> *21-23 For even hereunto were ye called: because Christ also suffered for us, leaving us an example, that ye should follow his steps: Who did no sin, neither was guile found in his mouth: Who, when he was reviled, reviled not again; when he suffered, he threatened not; but committed himself to him that judgeth righteously:*

What was this chapter talking about? It was expressing what a believer's response should be when they found themselves suffering physically for Christ's sake. It says in verse 19 that they should *endure grief*. These words mean to bear bravely and calmly the things that cause sorrow.

In contrast, Christ's response to undeserved suffering is highlighted in verses 21-23. They disclose that He didn't react to the mistreatment in a humanistic manner but verse 23 says that He *committed himself* to the Father. This means that Jesus gave judgement to the Father.

And not only so, do you remember the words He spoke when He was on the cross in Luke 23:34; His words were *Father, forgive them*. The word *forgive* means to give up a debt. It can also mean that those responsible for his crucifixion were not be punished along with not holding their actions against them with a view toward their salvation.

So, if we were to define the word healed from the context, it could mean to be set free from retaliation due to undeserved suffering by giving the matter over to God. Another way we could say this is that Christ suffered so that it would be possible for Christians to follow His steps, both in suffering and in righteous living.[160] Could we say that the word *healed* means that God sees us as being righteous in living. What do you think?

In our search, we found three possible renderings of the word *healed*: spiritual healing, physical healing or righteous in living. Is there one that seems to describe this word in the phrase *by whose stripes were ye healed?*

With that said, we could surmise that as Christ committed all suffering to God the Father, likewise, when you believed the gospel, you were healed, i.e., you're someone who evidences righteous living amidst undeserved suffering in the eyes of God. And subsequently, you should see yourself as being righteous in living, which evidences a godly testimony no matter what comes your way.

The next spiritual blessing that I'd like to introduce to you is similar to something that I'm sure many people would like to obtain with respect to the US. Any idea what I'm referring to?

27

YOU ARE A CITIZEN OF HEAVEN

Have you ever visited a specific country and wanted to become a citizen? In 2012, I volunteered with over six hundred people worldwide to participate in a building project sponsored by Habitat for Humanity. The goal was to build slightly more than one hundred small single-family homes in Leogane, Haiti.

I'd never traveled internationally before, let alone to Haiti. I had no idea what to expect. After attending a "get to know" dinner in Atlanta, Ga., the following day, all of us flew to Port au Prince airport. From there, we took a bus to the sight where we'd be lodging. I was expecting to stay at a grand hotel. However, when we arrived, I noticed hundreds of small tents set up. The only other time I stayed in a tent was when I was a boy scout. Each one of them would hold up to three or four people and was furnished with state-of-the-art sleeping arrangements, i.e., individual cots.

Breakfast would be served every morning at 6:00 a.m. From there, many buses would transport all of us to the building site. When we got there, I noticed over one hundred concrete slabs whose dimensions reflected the size (between one hundred to one hundred forty-four square feet) of each small house that was to be built. Most of the materials needed to construct the four exterior walls and roof were on site. In most cases, groups of ten-twelve people were assigned to complete the building of four houses, with one of the workers being designated as the supervisor. A young Irishman, who owned a business in Dublin, Ireland, was assigned to us.

The days were long, anywhere from ten-twelve hours in the intense heat of 95º F with extreme humidity. I found the need to drink water frequently as I'd usually go through at least ten bottles of water daily. As the days went on, it dawned on me that I hadn't gone to the bathroom. I thought there was something wrong with me. So, I called my wife and told her about this. And she said that I was probably sweating it out.

When it came time to return to where we stayed, we boarded the buses and looked forward to taking a shower. Two separate shower complexes with individual stalls for males and females had been previously built to accommodate about twenty of us at one time. Well, you can imagine, if you didn't run to your tent and gather your change of clothes quickly, you'd be in line for quite a while.

Little did I know that the shower water wasn't cool but ice cold. And there was no hot water option nearby. I soon became aware of something else that, caught my upmost attention, i.e., at times, there would be giant tarantulas waiting for you when you entered the shower enclosure. After cleaning up and putting on clean clothes, a buffet was waiting for us in the nearby food hall. Irish men and women did most of the cooking and serving. The food was quite good.

After dinner, there would be some kind of entertainment venue for us to enjoy. On one occasion, locals set up tables with homemade craft items for sale. Another night consisted of watching slides containing pictures of the various houses being built along with the volunteers involved with building them. And then there was the music night when those with a talent for singing and playing musical instruments performed before us all with two unexpected, surprising guests showing up, i.e., country singer songwriter Garth Brooks and Trisha Yearwood.

When the trip ended, I was looking forward to getting back home to the country where I was born as a citizen of the USA. As we traveled throughout Haiti, I noticed the immense amount of poverty everywhere. Many people lived in wooden shacks with dirt floors and no running water. Bathrooms were almost non-existent in certain areas of the country. Many people bathed or went to the bathroom in man-made ravines whose water source came from the nearby mountains.

While some cars were on the roads, most people either walked or rode mopeds. As for work, most of the population sold various items along the main streets of the towns or cities that we passed through. At the trip's close, each of us was asked if we wanted to donate any of our clothes or carpentry tools that we'd brought, which would be given to the new homeowners of the development. Most of us gave away just about all that we brought with us.

This brings me to this question. Would I want to live there? My honest answer is absolutely not. I'm so thankful that I'm a US citizen. Sometimes, we don't really know what we have until we go to another country and find out what they don't have.

So, what about you? Are you satisfied with your citizenship, wherever that might be? Do you wish there was a better place waiting for you where you could become a citizen of that country instead? Well, if you're a follower of Christ, there is. The book of Ephesians will tell us more about this.

Ephesians 2:19

> *Now therefore ye are no more strangers and foreigners, but fellowcitizens with the saints, and of the household of God;*

The Gentile Ephesians believers *are no more strangers* (of one who comes from another country or city and settles in another, but does not rank as a citizen)[161] *and foreigners* (guests in a private family, as opposed to the members of the family) *but fellowcitizens* (citizens of heaven) *with the saints* (Christianized Jews), *and of the household* (having all equal rights, privileges, and advantages; as all, through one Spirit[162]) *of God.*

The verb *are* in Koine Greek is in the form of a present active indicative. What this tells us is that all of those Gentiles who believed in Jesus are without interruption an inhabitant of heaven and of the same spiritual lineage with their fellow Jewish Christians.

In this world, depending on what country we live in, there will always be degrees of discontentment with the political system, human rights violations, the results of high-profile criminal trials, the lack of affordable housing, racial discrimination, unaffordable health care, limited employment opportunities, etc. However, Scripture tells us that there's a place called heaven where these conditions don't exist. Here's some of what we're told awaits us when we arrive there.

Revelations 21:4b...and there shall be no more death, neither sorrow, nor crying, neither shall there be any more pain: for the former things are passed away.

Right off the bat, we're reminded that there will *be no more death*. No one will ever die there. We'll live in a heavenly realm with those who've responded to the gospel. I hope with all my heart this includes my kids, relatives, friends and frankly the whole world. We're also told that there will no longer be any *sorrow* or *crying*. These are interesting words. The word *sorrow* means that there won't be any keen (intense) mental suffering or distress over affliction or loss.[163] And the word *crying* means that there will be no outbursts of grief. In other words, whatever would cause mental suffering or outbursts of heartache, such as loss of property or loved ones, persecution, regrets, etc., won't exist.

And finally, we're instructed that there will be no *more pain*. The word *pain* refers to the experience of pain, normally involving both continuity and intensity.[164] No one there will ever get sick physically or will experience bodily injuries. From this, we can deduce that there will no longer be any wars, extreme weather, pandemics, incurable diseases, physical handicaps, societal violence, etc.

You, like me, and all those who have put their trust in Christ have a literal place waiting for us to inhabit that is without comprehension. *As for now, you can proclaim that you're a resident of heaven with countless Christians along with being spiritually related to them.* Amen.

28

YOU ARE GOD'S INHERITANCE

Have you ever wished that you were born into a different family? I did. As the only child, I witnessed my father verbally and physically abuse my mother on infrequent occasions. While the physical abuse was limited, the verbal abuse seemed to occur on a daily basis for this or that.

As I got older, I became used to being yelled at for reasons that seemed inconsequential. There was one occasion when my father bought dinner for the family. With anticipation, I couldn't wait to see what he ordered. To my surprise, it was something I'd never seen before. It was called scallops. Just looking at them made my skin crawl. They had this weird looking finish on their surface. Almost like the same one when someone looks at uncooked chicken.

I was told in no uncertain terms to eat it. So, I bit into one of them and swallowed. All of a sudden, I ran to the bathroom and threw up into the toilet. And so, the angry response from my father ensued.

It appeared that he was always on edge. There was reason to assume that something would happen that would spark the flame. When we'd visit his brother or one of his five sisters, their households always appeared to be welcoming, calm, and loving. My cousins seemed to enjoy being home and interacting with both parents. I wished we could change places.

How about you? What was your home life like? Do you wish you belonged to a different family?

Did you know that some children have no parents to go home to? The reasons for such a dire situation vary. Both parents died. A single parent couldn't afford to keep them. Displacement due to war separated them. Alcohol or drug abuse caused the parent to abandon them. Ever wonder what happens to them? It really depends on what country they were born in. Let me provide you with an article that provides alarming statistics concerning this plight.

ORPHAN AND CHILD POVERTY FACT SHEET

[It's] estimated that there are over 100 million orphans worldwide (UNICEF). To give you an idea of the enormity of the [numbers,] compare it with the population of the United [States, which is just a little over 325 million,] or the current population of Russia -145 million. Over 100 million children would equal the combined populations of New York City, Los Angles, [Chicago, and 47 of] the largest cities in the USA, plus the combined populations of Ireland, Norway, Denmark, France, [Greece, Nicaragua, and Costa Rica. These aren't] just numbers and [statistics;] these are CHILDREN! - distressed, [struggling,] and with little hope in the world.

According to UNICEF, almost [5,700] children become orphans every day due to war, natural [disasters,] poverty, disease, [stigma,] and medical needs.

According to the World Health Organization (WHO), in 2017, 15,000 children under the age of 5 died every day; that is equivalent to 1 child every 17 seconds. 2.7 million children die every year in the first month of life.

Every 15 seconds, another child becomes an AIDS orphan in [Africa.]

60% of orphan girls will become victims of the sex trade. 10-15%

[of] orphan children will commit suicide before age 18. 70% of orphan boys in Eastern Europe will become criminals.

250,000 children are adopted [annually,] but 14,050,000 orphan children will grow up and age out of the orphan care system without ever having been part of a loving family. That means that every day 38,493 children will age out of an orphanage. That's one orphan every 2.2 seconds who will leave an orphanage or foster care with no family to belong to and no place to call home. Less than 1% of all orphan children will be adopted. Who will care for the rest of the millions of orphaned, [abandoned,] and homeless children?

Russia – [It's estimated that since the fall of the Iron Curtain,] there are between 1 and 4 million homeless children in Russia. There are 30,000 children living on the streets and in the sewers and subways in Moscow (see the Google [video - "The Children of Leningradsky"). At around age of 16] or 17, orphans are forced to leave the orphanage system and enter the world with limited education and minimal support.

Within the first five years, almost 90% of these orphans end up in crime, prostitution, [drug, and alcohol addiction, or commit suicide. In Ukraine and [Russia,] 10% -15% of children who age out of an orphanage commit suicide before age 18; 60% of the girls are lured into prostitution; 70% of the boys become hardened criminals. Another Russian study reported that of the 15,000 orphans aging out of state-run institutions every year, 10% committed suicide, 5,000 were unemployed, 6,000 were [homeless,] and 3,000 were in prison within three years.

India - The orphan crisis in India is staggering. According to the United Nations Children's Fund (UNICEF), India has more than 29.6 million children living on the streets. Orphanages are filled with abandoned [children,] and millions more wander the streets just doing what they can to survive (see the movie: "Slumdog [Millionaire").]

. . .

Africa - Africa has an estimated 39 million orphans. Every year 2,102,400 more children become orphans in Africa alone. Every 15 seconds, another child in Africa becomes an AIDS orphan. There are an estimated 14 million AIDS orphans in Sub-Saharan Africa; 8 out of 10 children in Sub-Saharan Africa will be orphaned by AIDS (a number higher than the total of every [under-eighteen-year-old] in Canada, Norway, Sweden, Denmark, and Ireland combined). Uganda has over 17 million children, 15% of whom are orphans (2.5 million orphans). According to the UN, over 50% of Uganda's children under five suffer from malnutrition, and the country has a 60% child mortality rate. Thousands of West African children were orphaned by losing parents to Ebola in countries like Guinea, Liberia (where Orphans Lifeline International is working), and Sierra Leone.

Haiti has an estimated 1.2 million orphans and vulnerable children (OVC). About 7,000 children roam the streets of Port-au-Prince. Thousands more can be found across the island in cities such as Cap Haitien and Gonaives. Over 6 million Haitians live below the poverty line on less than [$2.41 USD] per day, and more than 2.5 million are below the extreme poverty line of [$1.23 USD] per day.

Every week hundreds of babies and children are abandoned in Haiti shortly after birth. They are left in hospitals, shop doorways, alleys or simply dumped in the street. Many are abandoned because their parents have no means to feed and take care of them. A large number of children become orphaned because their parents have died from disease, natural [disasters], conflicts, and political turmoil. The January 2010 earthquake left tens of thousands of new orphan children in this impoverished nation that is only 600 miles from Miami, USA.[165]

I can't imagine this kind of existence. Can you? What awaits each and every one of us is the opportunity to belong to a family that will never stop loving us while making available the necessities of life for those who are their children. Would you like to hear more about this? Please turn to the book of Ephesians.

Ephesians 1:11

In whom also we have obtained an inheritance, being predestinated according to the purpose of him who worketh all things after the counsel of his own will:

The Jews, who are in Christ, have been made an inheritance. The verb *have obtained* in Koine Greek is in the Aorist Passive Indicative. At a point in time in the past, when they responded to the gospel, facts state that they received the spiritual blessing of becoming God's possession.

Likewise, you're God's heritage. At salvation, you've been born into the family of the Father, Son, and Holy Spirit, which contains millions of spiritual brothers and sisters. A whole new spiritual world awaits you. No longer will you be alone. No longer will people not care about you.

The next spiritual reality tells us that we're dead and yet alive. How can this be?

29

YOU ARE DEAD AND YOUR LIFE IS HID WITH CHRIST IN GOD

A few years back a new TV show came on the screen and captivated millions of people. I don't know if you ever heard of it and watched it. It was called *The Walking Dead*. The following articles tell us what this was all about.

THE WALKING DEAD (TV SERIES)

The Walking Dead is an American post-apocalyptic horror drama television series based on the comic book series of the same name by Robert Kirkman, Tony Moore, and Charlie Adlard—together forming the core of *The Walking Dead* franchise...

Series overview
Main article: List of The Walking Dead episodes
[*The Walking Dead*] takes place after the onset of a worldwide zombie apocalypse. The [zombies referred to as "walkers,"] shamble toward living humans and other creatures to eat them; they are attracted to noise, such as gunshots, [and different scents, e.g.,]

humans. Although it initially seems that only humans that are bitten or scratched by walkers can turn into other walkers, [it's] revealed early in the series that all living humans carry the pathogen responsible for the mutation. The mutation is activated after the death of the pathogen's host, and the only way to permanently kill a walker is to damage its brain or destroy the body entirely, such as by cremating it.

The series centers on sheriff's deputy Rick Grimes, who wakes up from a coma. While in a coma, the world has been taken over by walkers. He becomes the leader of a group of survivors from the Atlanta, Georgia, region as they attempt to sustain and protect themselves not only against attacks by walkers but by other groups of survivors willing to use any means necessary to stay alive.[166]

Zombie [Apocalypse]
   Origins

The myth of the zombie originated in Haiti in the 17th and 18th centuries when African slaves were brought in to work on sugar plantations under the rule of France. The slaves believed that if they ended their own lives by [suicide, they'd] be condemned to spend eternity trapped in their own bodies as the undead. This myth evolved in the Voodoo religion into the Haitian belief that corpses were reanimated by shamans.[167] The zombie concept eventually infiltrated western culture with the publication of the first example of zombie fiction in 1927, which was a book titled The Magic Island written by William Seabrook.[168]

Based on what we just read, another word we could use to characterize these people is called the undead. This word refers to someone [who's] no longer alive but animated by a supernatural force, as a vampire or zombie.[169] Did you know that in Christ you are also dead? However, you are also alive. This doesn't seem to make sense, but it does. Let's find out what this is all about. Please go to the book of Colossians.

. . .

Colossians 3:3-4

> *For ye are dead, and your life is hid with Christ in God. When Christ, who is our life, shall appear, then shall ye also appear with him in glory.*

The Apostle Paul conveyed to the Colossians believers that they *are dead*. It's obvious that this doesn't mean physical death as they were yet alive when he spoke to them. The word *dead* in Koine Greek means so far as your spiritual being is concerned, you died which means you were separated from the former life and everything of an evil nature that pertained to it.[170] And their new *life* (true life; risen life) is *hid* (concealed; has not yet been revealed) *with Christ in God*. However, when Christ does return to the earth, you shall be with Him.

In your position with Christ, your old life no longer exists. You're, in fact, a new creation. You're no longer the person you used to be. Yes, you will be reminded of this or that by your memories, your friends, family, etc. However, your new spiritual life is no longer in the sphere of the earthly and sensual but is with the life of the risen Christ.[171]

So, set your mind to learn and apply all the things of Christ, e.g., His person and work, the foundational teachings of the Christian faith, and the divine truths about how we should think differently about ourselves, others, and the circumstances of life so that the reality of your past life having ended will become more evident.

This concludes our study of becoming aware of all the blessings that have taken place in the spirit of your life when you responded to the gospel of Christ. Whatever these blessings declare, God sees you as such. They're irrevocable. There's nothing you, someone, or something else could do to remove any of them from you. So, be thankful and remind yourself of them from time to time.

What I'd like to do now is leave you with some closing words.

RICH IN CHRIST

I never knew how rich I am in Christ until now. For years, I always tried to perform religiously to be righteous, be approved, be sanctified, etc., in the eyes of church leadership. This doesn't mean that we shouldn't learn how to work out in our experience the new standing that we have in Christ.

Philippians 2:12

> *Wherefore, my beloved, as ye have always obeyed, not as in*
> *my presence only, but now much more in my absence,*
> *work out your own salvation with fear and trembling.*

We're instructed to *work out* (to put into practice in their daily [living,] what God had worked in them by His Spirit[172]) our own *salvation* (carry their salvation to its ultimate conclusion, namely, Christlikeness, i.e., maintain victory over sin and the living of a life pleasing to the Lord Jesus[173]).

As we reflect on the divine declarations about us, our new lives in Christ will not only become realized in our experience, but we'll begin to recognize teachings, whether they support God's view of us. Don't allow anyone to say that you must do this or that to obtain these spiritual realities. And if someone says you can lose because of thus or such, run baby run.

And don't forget, you also have another adversary who'll try to convince you that you're not such as you believe you are.

1 Peter 5:8-9

> *Be sober, be vigilant; because your adversary the devil, as a roaring lion, walketh about, seeking whom he may devour: Whom resist stedfast in the faith, knowing that the same afflictions are accomplished in your brethren that are in the world.*

We're told to *be sober* (mentally self-controlled), and *vigilant* (awake and watchful; never be off your guard), because our *adversary* (opponent), *the devil*, is trying to *devour* (destroy) us by beguiling our senses, perverting our judgment; enchanting our imaginations; deceiving us with false views of spiritual things; and destroying us with violent opposition, persecution, and death.

Whom we are to *resist* (withstand) by being *stedfast* (rocklike firmness) *in the faith* (trust in a body of doctrine or beliefs which Christians adhere to along with depending upon the strengthening and protecting power of God).

So, as you begin to think of yourself in the right way, i.e., according to God's Word, your view of others and responses to the circumstances of life will change. And people will begin to see you as the new "I am," as you automatically evidence what the following verse expresses what God's desire is for all of us.

> *Acts 1:8b ... and ye shall be witnesses unto me both in Jerusalem, and in all Judaea, and in Samaria, and unto the uttermost part of the earth.*

I hope you enjoyed reading this study as much as I did while writing it. I'd appreciate it if you could leave a review on Amazon. Thank you and God Bless.

ENDNOTES

[1] Calvin's Commentaries Pc Study Bible version 5, 2006. BIBLESOFT. WEB. 15 September 2022
   <http://www.biblesoft.com>.

[2] Jamieson, Faucet, and Brown Commentary Pc Study Bible version 5, 2005. BIBLESOFT. WEB. 15 September 2022
   <http://www.biblesoft.com>.

[3] The Pulpit Commentary Pc Study Bible version 5, 2006. BIBLESOFT. WEB. 13 November 2022
   <http://www.biblesoft.com>.

[4] Bible Knowledge Commentary/New Testament Copyright © 1983, 2000 Cook Communications Ministries. BIBLESOFT. WEB. 29 September 2022
   <http://www.biblesoft.com>.

[5] Bible Knowledge Commentary/New Testament.

[6] Barnes' Notes. Pc Study Bible version 5, 2006. BIBLESOFT. WEB. 29 September 2022
   <http://www.biblesoft.com>.

[7] "What is salvation?" 18 September 2022
   <http://www.riverpower.org/answers/salvation.htm>.

ENDNOTES

[8] Weust's Word Studies from the Greek New Testament Pc Study Bible version 5, 2005.

[9] Barnes' Notes.

[10] Keil and Delitzsch Commentary on the Old Testament Pc Study Bible version 5, 2005.

[11] Keil and Delitzsch Commentary.

[12] Barnes' Notes.

[13] The Pulpit Commentary.

[14] The Pulpit Commentary.

[15] Jamieson, Faucet, and Brown Commentary.

[16] Jamieson, Faucet, and Brown Commentary.

[17] The Bible Exposition Commentary/New Testament.

[18] The Bible Exposition Commentary/New Testament.

[19] The Pulpit Commentary.

[20] Vincent's New Testament Word Studies Pc Study Bible version 5, 2005. BIBLESOFT. WEB. 6 October 2022 <http://www.biblesoft.com>.

[21] Vincent's New Testament Word Studies.

[22] Adam Clarke's Commentary.

[23] The Bible Exposition Commentary/New Testament.

[24] Weust's Word Studies.

[25] Weust's Word Studies.

[26] Weust's Word Studies.

[27] Weust's Word Studies.

[28] Jamieson, Faucet, and Brown Commentary.

[29] Weust's Word Studies.

[30] Weust's Word Studies.

[31] Weust's Word Studies.

[32] Adam Clarke's Commentary.

[33] Barnes' Notes.

[34] Dictionary.com.

[35] Exegetical Dictionary of the New Testament Pc Study Bible version 5, 2005. BIBLESOFT. WEB. 21 October 2022 <http://www.biblesoft.com>.

ENDNOTES

36 IVP Bible Background Commentary Pc Study Bible version 5, 2005. BIBLESOFT. WEB. 22 October 2022 <http://www.biblesoft.com>.

37 Weust's Word Studies.

38 The Pulpit Commentary.

39 Barnes' Notes.

40 Adam Clarke's Commentary.

41 Barnes' Notes.

42 The Bible Exposition Commentary/New Testament.

43 Jamieson, Faucet, and Brown Commentary.

44 Weust's Word Studies.

45 Weust's Word Studies.

46 Adam Clarke's Commentary.

47 UBS New Testament Handbook Series Pc Study Bible version 5, 2005. BIBLESOFT. WEB. 27 October 2022 <http://www.biblesoft.com>.

48 UBS New Testament.

49 The Online Bible Thayer's Greek Lexicon and Brown Driver & Briggs Hebrew Lexicon, Copyright © 1993, Woodside Bible Fellowship, Ontario, Canada. Licensed from the Institute for Creation Research.

50 Bible Knowledge Commentary/New Testament.

51 The Bible Exposition Commentary/New Testament.

52 Wuest Word Studies.

53 Wuest Word Studies.

54 Wuest's Word Studies.

55 Wuest's Word Studies.

56 UBS New Testament.

57 Calvin's Commentaries.

58 UBS New Testament.

59 Barnes' Notes.

60 UBS New Testament.

61 Weust's Word Studies.

62 Weust's Word Studies.

63 Jamieson, Fausset, and Brown Commentary.

ENDNOTES

[64] The Bible Exposition Commentary/New Testament.
[65] IVP Bible Background Commentary.
[66] The Bible Exposition Commentary/New Testament.
[67] Weust's Word Studies.
[68] Bible Knowledge Commentary//New Testament.
[69] Barnes' Notes.
[70] Jamieson, Faucet, and Brown Commentary.
[71] Weust's Word Studies.
[72] "Black Death," *History* 6 December 2022 <https://bit.ly/2CWFWKO>.
[73] Weust's Word Studies.
[74] The Pulpit Commentary.
[75] "WHAT IS BONDED [LABOR]?" *anti-slavery* 27 November 2022 <https://bit.ly/2SrOYI0>.
[76] Barnes' Notes.
[77] The Pulpit Commentary.
[78] Weust's Word Studies.
[79] Bible Knowledge Commentary/New Testament.
[80] Bible Knowledge Commentary/New Testament.
[81] "SURVIVING LEPROSY: A STORY OF GRACE," *map international* 15 November 2022 <https://bit.ly/3EbXK1S>.
[82] The Pulpit Commentary.
[83] The Pulpit Commentary.
[84] Wuest's Word Studies.
[85] Jamieson, Fausset, and Brown Commentary.
[86] "Who becomes a saint in the Catholic Church, and is that changing?" *THE CONVERSATION* 03 November 2022 <https://bit.ly/3T3llBy>.
[87] The Pulpit Commentary.
[88] Jamieson, Fausset, and Brown Commentary.
[89] "How did Bruce Lee die," *yourdictionary* 17 November 2022 <https://bit.ly/3ALnyRF>.
[90] UBS New Testament.
[91] Bible Knowledge Commentary/New Testament.

ENDNOTES

[92] The Bible Exposition Commentary.

[93] "Free to Succeed: Naomi Blount," *FAMM* 3 November 2022 <https://famm.org/stories/free-to-succeed-naomi-blount/>.

[94] Bible Knowledge Commentary/New Testament.

[95] IVP Bible Background Commentary.

[96] Jamieson, Faucet, and Brown Commentary.

[97] UBS New Testament.

[98] Adam Clarke's Commentary.

[99] Barnes' Notes.

[100] Barnes' Notes.

[101] Barnes' Notes.

[102] UBS New Testament.

[103] UBS New Testament.

[104] Weust's Word Studies.

[105] Weust's Word Studies.

[106] Dictionary.com.

[107] Jim Avila, Geoff Martz and Joanne Napolitano. "ONLINE LOVE TRIANGLE, DECEPTION END IN MURDER," *abc NEWS* 27 November 2022 <https://abcn.ws/3u2sFZV>.

[108] UBS New Testament.

[109] Calvin's Commentaries.

[110] Calvin's Commentaries.

[111] Adam Clarke's Commentary.

[112] Adam Clarke's Commentary.

[113] Barnes' Notes.

[114] Dictionary.com.

[115] Jamieson, Fausset, and Brown Commentary.

[116] "Grave bells indicated 'the deceased' were alive," *The Parkersburg News & Sentinel* 4 December 2022 <https://bit.ly/3VwtBl4>.

[117] New Exhaustive Strong's Numbers and Concordance with Expanded Greek-Hebrew Dictionary. Copyright © 1994, 2003, 2006 Biblesoft, Inc. and International Bible Translators, Inc; 25 November 2022

ENDNOTES

<http://www.biblesoft.com>.

[118] Bible Knowledge Commentary/New Testament.

[119] IVP Bible Background Commentary.

[120] Wuest's Word Studies.

[121] Barnes' Notes.

[122] "What are the current statistics on divorce?" 20 November 2022 <https://bit.ly/3hYyOU7>.

[123] Dannah Gresh. "HOW TO GET LOST IN GOD'S LOVE AND SAVE YOUR MARRIAGE" *FOCUS ON THE FAMILY* 19 November 2022 <https://bit.ly/3Atz57M>.

[124] The Pulpit Commentary.

[125] The Bible Exposition Commentary/New Testament.

[126] Weust's Word Studies.

[127] Weust's Word Studies.

[128] The Bible Exposition Commentary.

[129] Bible Knowledge Commentary//New Testament.

[130] Thayer's Greek Lexicon and Brown Driver & Briggs Hebrew Lexicon.

[131] Calvin's Commentaries.

[132] Weust's Word Studies.

[133] Jamieson, Faucet, and Brown Commentary.

[134] Adam Clarke's Commentary.

[135] Barnes' Notes.

[136] Calvin's Commentaries.

[137] Cynthis Measom. "A $180K POKÉMON CARD AND THE GEEKIEST STUFF THAT COULD MAKE YOU RICH," 6 November 2022 <https://bit.ly/3zK6FWY>.

[138] Jamieson, Faucet, and Brown Commentary.

[139] Wuest's Word Studies.

[140] Wuest's Word Studies.

[141] Vincent's New Testament Word Studies.

[142] Barnes' Notes.

[143] Bible Knowledge Commentary/New Testament.

[144] Bible Knowledge Commentary/New Testament.

[145] "Spider-Man," 22 November 2022 <https://en.wikipedia.org/wiki/Spider-Man>.

[146] The Pulpit Commentary.

[147] UBS New Testament Handbook Series.

[148] Lester Sumrall. "The Gifts and Ministries of the Holy Spirit." Lester Sumrall Evangelical Association, 1982.

[149] "How to Become a US Ambassador," *BAU* 4 November 2022 <https://bau.edu/blog/how-to-become-a-u-s-ambassador/>.

[150] The Pulpit Commentary.

[151] Megan D. Robinson. "A Brief History of the Mona Lisa, the World's Most Famous Painting," *Art&object* 3 December 2022 <https://bit.ly/3FlsFdR>.

[152] Bible Knowledge Commentary/New Testament.

[153] The Bible Exposition Commentary/New Testament.

[154] "Michelle's Story," *nami* 7 December 2022 <https://bit.ly/3VH21lt>.

[155] Jamieson, Fausset, and Brown Commentary.

[156] Barnes' Notes.

[157] Barnes' Notes.

[158] Barnes' Notes.

[159] UBS New Testament Handbook Series.

[160] Bible Knowledge Commentary//New Testament.

[161] Wuest's Word Studies.

[162] Adam Clarke's Commentary.

[163] Dictionary.com.

[164] Greek-English Lexicon Pc Study Bible version 5, 2005. BIBLESOFT. WEB. 27 November 2022 <https://biblesoft.com>.

[165] "Orphan and Child Poverty Fact Sheet," *ORPHAN'S LIFELINE INT'L* 06 March 2023 <https://bit.ly/3ygyUv7>.

[166] "The Walking Dead (TV series)" *Wikipedia* 06 February 2023 <https://bit.ly/3YvCE6t>.

ENDNOTES

[167]Mariani, Mike (October 28, 2015). "The Tragic, Forgotten History of Zombies," *The Atlantic*. Retrieved November 2, 2022. <https://bit.ly/3ZKQgfb>.
[168]"Zombie apocalypse," *Wikipedia* 06 February 2023 <https://bit.ly/3mu2Scm>.
[169]Dictionary.com.
[170]Weust's Word Studies.
[171]Vincent's Word Studies.
[172]Bible Knowledge Commentary/New Testament.
[173]Weust's Word Studies.

Made in the USA
Middletown, DE
04 April 2023

27918689R00096